ARCHITECTURE
MATTERS

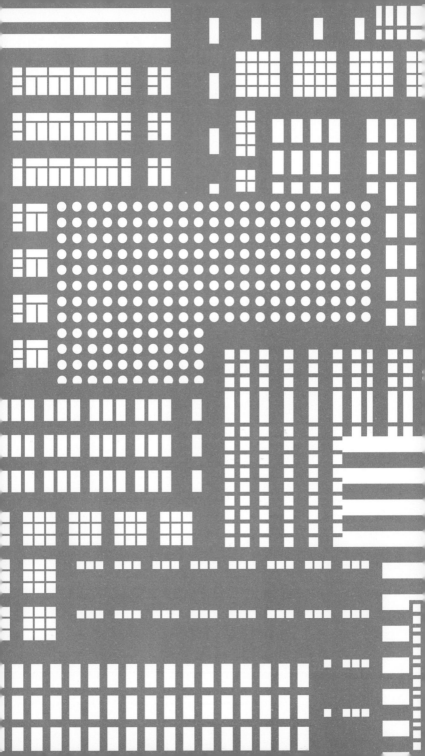

ARCHITECTURE MATTERS

AARON BETSKY

Thames & Hudson

PREFACE

I have an addictive personality. Luckily, my main vice is architecture. I get up in the morning and surf architecture sites. I look at architecture all day long (luckily, I work at Taliesin and Taliesin West, two Frank Lloyd Wright sites that fulfill my needs on a daily basis), talk about architecture incessantly, teach it, write about it, and argue about it until it is time to go to bed. When I travel, I visit sites of great architecture and try to see the latest constructions, immersing myself in whatever beautiful or intriguing spaces I can.

About the only thing I do not do is make architecture in the traditional sense. Instead, I make books like this, write articles, lecture, and teach. I have tried to be a designer, and like to think I was pretty good at it, but I quickly learned that my talents were more as a scrivener, a critic, an editor, and one who could help a student figure out just how to make a good design better.

What I have done instead of sitting at a drafting table is to gather together images and ideas—mainly from and about architecture, but also from art and art history, philosophy, and other areas—string them together, layer them, cut through them with (mis)interpretations, and then weave together theories about why architecture matters.

But you can't learn to love architecture or figure out why it matters just from abstractions. I LEARNED TO LOVE ARCHITECTURE BY EXPERIENCING BUILDINGS, SITES, INTERIORS, AND IMAGES. I travel around the world because I am asked to give lectures or otherwise to contribute to some part of the architecture culture, but in truth it is so that I can experience places that human beings have transformed into spaces for human appearance. Nothing gives me greater pleasure than to see a beautiful building or to walk a site where human and natural beauty come together. It is that experience I want to share here, but also to encourage you as a reader to have for yourself. GO OUT AND FIND A BUILDING. HUG A COLUMN, WANDER THROUGH A CITY, OR IMMERSE YOURSELF IN AN ENVIRONMENT CRAFTED TO TAKE YOU TO ANOTHER PLACE.

Luckily, you don't always have to travel in real life. Films, videos, and good, old-fashioned books have the same power to transport us into a new reality. Improve your carbon footprint and snuggle up with a good novel or a movie. A lot of this book is the result of my having spent a great deal of time doing exactly that.

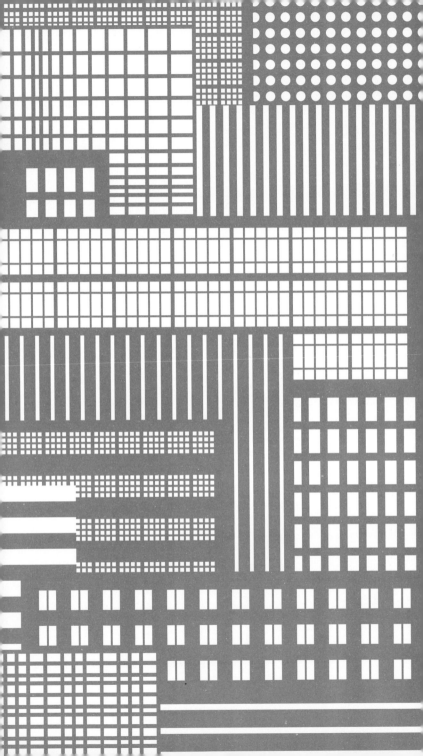

46 THOUGHTS ON

WHY ARCHITECTURE MATTERS

WHY ARCHITECTURE IS SO COOL (TO A TEENAGER)

1 It all started with tea at Mrs. Schroeder's. I was in high school in a small village in the Netherlands, where I had moved with my parents and sister when I was four years old from, of all places, Missoula, Montana. I had been given a classroom assignment to write an essay about an art movement that was named after the magazine it published, *De Stijl* (The Style). Its most famous proponent was the artist Piet Mondrian, whose paintings evolved into squares and rectangles in primary colors, caught in a web of black lines he carefully calibrated, like the whole composition, to have what he felt was just the right width and run. I tried hard to understand these abstractions, but they were, well, abstract.

"You know, there is a house that is like a three-dimensional Mondrian," my teacher said, sensing my frustration with the flat pictures; "a friend of mine owns it, you should go see it." She arranged a visit, and one sunny spring day I mounted my bicycle and rode the almost nine kilometers to the house. As I approached the building, I cycled along a row of houses clad in brick, like almost every neighborhood in the Netherlands I knew. Then the row stopped and gave way to a single white line, then a deep recess held by a horizontal plane at the top, a yellow strip running along its front, and a red strip behind it, with a balcony intersecting the

shadow and connecting to a white wall with no windows, no doors,
and no details to give away its scale.

I was somewhat perplexed. I dismounted, parked my bicycle along
the fence of white posts, and saw that the rhythm of planes and
lines continued on the house's other side, pushing and pulling at
whatever volume was hiding inside. I understood what my teacher
meant, and I also saw the skeleton of the row of houses next door,
their brick stripped away, their structure exposed and bleached.
This was not just a house: this was the scaffolding for a building,
or the building parts out of which something else could be
constructed. It was full of possibilities. It was also unfinished,
raw, and strangely so much more full of life than its staid neighbors.

Later, I found out that the elevated highway that stood right next
to the house had not been there when the building was finished in
1924; instead, the planes had dissolved the urban forms into the
geometry of meadows and irrigation ditches that marked what
was then open country.

I opened the gate, walked in, and rang the doorbell, noticing the
small bench where, I found out later, the friends of Mrs. Schroeder's
son used to come and sit while they talked to him through the
window opening into his small room on the ground floor.

Mrs. Schroeder, by then in her eighties, opened the door and took
me upstairs.

The world fell apart. I had no words for the complexity of what I
encountered. The stair arrived in the middle of the second floor, where
the game of planes continued, but now in bright colors. There was a
red piece of floor and a blue one, and then a blue part of the ceiling
and a yellow strip running overhead. Soon it became clear how it all

worked. Mrs. Schroeder began moving walls, and as she did so the one large room became two rooms, then three, and then four, leaving only the staircase open. Each space, once it was closed, contained its own planes coming together or spinning apart to shape the room without making any objects.

What things there were, whether built-in cabinets or chairs, sofas, desks, and tables, were of the same design. The house's architect, Gerrit Rietveld, had been a furniture designer whom Mrs. and Mr. Schroeder had hired to redo the interior of their jewelry store. The house was the first of many buildings he went on to design, but he was just as famous for compositions such as the "Red Blue Chair," two angled slats in red and blue held in a network of black-painted sticks with yellow tips.

So this was architecture. You could make a space that could change according to how you used it, or whether you wanted to be alone or in company. You could mark and measure each plane and piece of space so that you always knew your body in relation to its surroundings. You could make a home for yourself that was radically modern, even fifty years after it had been built.

"All this moving around has made me hot," Mrs. Schroeder said. "Shall we have some tea? Here, sit down at the table there in the corner." I followed her suggestion and was just looking outside when she reached over, turned a latch, and opened each window that met at the corner. Suddenly, the edge disappeared. I felt as if all the space in the room escaped into the garden and all the space outside rushed into the room.

I WAS HOOKED. IF YOU COULD DO THAT WITH ARCHITEC-TURE, I WANTED TO BE AN ARCHITECT.

In the end, I never did become an architect. I studied architecture, not only by visiting as many buildings as I could, but also in a formal manner, earning a Master of Architecture degree. I worked for several architects and opened my own practice, but I never obtained a license and, ultimately, decided that what I loved most was to do what I am doing right now: sharing my enthusiasm for all that architecture can do and be.

HOW TO BUILD AN (ELITE) COMMUNITY

2 I went to college at Yale University, a prestigious or self-important institution (depending on your perspective) that just happened to have a strong emphasis on architecture. When I arrived there as a freshman, I found myself in a fairytale world of neo-Gothic and neo-colonial structures, with a few modern buildings interrupting the idyll. I thought it was all rather strange and otherworldly at first, but then became more and more intrigued by the buildings that surrounded me, to the point that the first book I published was a monograph on the architect who designed most of those buildings. It was through my research on that designer that I began to define what interested me about architecture beyond the beauty of making spaces.

His name was James Gamble Rogers, and his story and that of his involvement with Yale made me realize how architecture can operate to create another world, one that is not just physical, but that through its presence, its imagery, and its spaces offers a vision of how we can build a community together. In cases such as Yale, it takes a lot of money to do so, but you can apply the principles to many other situations.

Rogers was born in rural Kentucky but moved to Chicago as a child. Though he was not from a particularly wealthy family, he was smart enough to obtain a scholarship to Yale but, while he was there, he spent so much energy having a good time he was almost kicked out. He returned to Chicago and went to work as an architect, even though there is no evidence of him having had any interest in or knowledge of the field. The city was booming, and he quickly built up an office with quite a few commissions. Apparently growing up and becoming ambitious enough to feel that he needed some formal training, he left his practice to his brother and took off to Paris, where he received the old-fashioned architectural schooling he lacked. When he returned, he married into one of Chicago's most powerful families, designed houses, office buildings, and schools, and eventually moved to New York, working around the country.

What really made Rogers's career was the 1917 commission to design the Memorial Quadrangle at his alma mater. Finished in 1921, the building was essentially a dormitory complex for the fast-growing campus. It was also a memorial for Charles Harkness, son of one of America's richest men—John D. Rockefeller's lawyer and business partner. Through this commission, or perhaps before it, Rogers came to know Charles's brother, Edward, who inherited most of the family money and proceeded to give it away over the course of his life.

Edward Harkness's largesse consisted principally of commissioning buildings for schools, universities, and, later, hospitals. Whenever he did commission, Rogers was the architect.

Starting in 1924, client and architect conspired with the then President of Yale, James Rowland Angell, to reshape Yale College into residential colleges, and this where Rogers really came into his own.

Each of the eventual twelve colleges was based on the model Rogers developed in the Memorial Quadrangle, which itself was divided up into two of the first units, Branford and Saybrook. I lived in Branford, and I remember sitting in its central courtyard, realizing what a place apart it was. The Memorial Tower served as a beacon proclaiming its importance to the wider world. A smaller tower on the opposite end of the courtyard was a replica of the parish church where the college's first benefactor, Elihu Yale, had worshipped. From the turrets, the faces of famous poets and philosophers peered down, acting as mirrors of what we aspired to be. All around me, the rows of college dorm rooms hid behind stone façades whose intricacy drew your eye forward, and whose towers, cross gables, projecting eaves, dormer windows, and passageways broke down the mass of what was basically a steel-framed residential block. The large courtyard gathered us together, while smaller versions of this central space gave identity to groups of rooms and roommates. Anchoring the whole was what looked like the nave of a church, but was actually a dining hall sitting on top of a row of living rooms where we could gather to read or talk.

In doing my research on the college system, I soon learned there was a logic to all of this. Harkness, Rogers, and Angell felt that the college was becoming too large and too diverse. They felt the need to create a community, one that could take (in those days only) men from different backgrounds, gather them together, and give them a place to study, play, and live that would be so shaped as to imbue them with a shared set of values. Some of that work of molding future minds and networks happened through the spaces that brought the young men together, some of it happened through inscriptions chiseled above the entry ways, and some of it happened through the way in which the buildings appeared. Rogers went around Europe, collecting postcards from Oxford and Cambridge, but also from monasteries and cloisters in France, which he then collaged together to give the sense that this was a place that had a tradition going back to the Middle Ages, even though it was brand new. He went as far as to write an instruction into the documents used to construct the Quadrangle that specified that every now and then workmen should break and repair a pane of glass before installing it, so that the building would look used and abused on the day it opened.

This was architecture that used scientific construction, research, and organization to create a completely artificial place. It worked. By the time I attended Yale fifty years later, it was so steeped in history it might as well have been medieval, while it worked so well in shaping men into a shared set of values that even I, an ornery, lefty radical with long hair, soon became a "true blue son of Eli."

What made it all the more remarkable was that Rogers made architecture in a thoroughly modern manner. He did not, as far as I was able to tell, design every building. Instead, he was an impresario, somebody who had the social connections (through marriage), the wit, and the charm to obtain commissions, as well as the business acumen to get them constructed. He also surrounded himself with talented renderers who could create seductive images; craftspeople who could execute the designs; and specialists in just about every area needed to create a convincing and inhabitable fantasy.

The buildings were of a piece, and they worked, but, more than that, they created that other place, separate from the world around it. In Rogers's realm, you lived in an architecture honed to be as strange, in its own way, as the Schroeder House was, but at a much larger scale and in a style that most people found familiar, if also not quite normal. Rogers and my four years at Yale convinced me that architecture did not have to be always weird, different, or startling. It could get under your skin and change you.

It also taught me one other important lesson: architecture works for those who can pay for it, and who want to see their vision of the world built.

HOW YOU CAN GET AWAY WITH DOING (ALMOST) NOTHING

3 It took a few years before I began to learn how you could sneak something different into the discipline I was then learning as a profession. I was twenty-two years old, I was on my first trip to Los Angeles, and I was staying with the man I considered to be one of the best architects of his generation, even if most people outside of California had never heard of him. Frank Gehry had been one of my teachers at the Yale School of Architecture and had invited me to stay with him for a few days in his house, which was already famous among architects and notorious in the town of Santa Monica.

Now he was walking me around his studio, a ramshackle affair steps away from the sea-breeze-blown carnival that was Venice Beach. He had only a dozen people working for him and a few projects, but one was particularly fascinating: the renovation of a former LA trolley-car barn into a temporary home for the nascent Museum of Contemporary Art. Gehry showed me the model of the building, pointing out how he was covering the bottom of the steel columns with stucco to protect them from fire, describing the ramps he was building and ... not much else. He saw me looking at the model and said: "Don't tell anybody, but I'm not really doing anything."

The first thing I learned from that short exchange is that every good architect is, at least a little bit, a politician. They make you feel special, in their confidence and in the know. You have their trust in a way others do not. I later found out that Gehry used the same line on everybody to whom he showed the model.

Yet the other lesson I learned was that the statement was, at least to a certain extent, true. Faced with a building that had large spaces appropriate for the scale of much contemporary art, but also with a small budget, Gehry added only minimal bits and pieces: he cleaned up the existing floors, walls, and ceilings, making sure they were structurally sound; he made stairs and ramps that allowed access to the various levels; and he put fireproofing up just as far as the building codes demanded. Then he worked with the curators to design freestanding white walls on which art could hang, and created a canopy to announce what was inside, along with a ticket booth. This was architecture that was minimal in its use of materials and new forms. Its effect was to reveal and accentuate what was already there. The big space, lit from above by skylights, was impressive in its own right and did not need much to make it better. The planes that enclosed it had the patina of age and the marks of an industrial expression in which connections such as bolts and screws were on display, so that you could understand the reality of the place and how it had been made.

> WHAT GEHRY DID WAS TO REVEAL THE BEAUTY OF THE HUMBLE, EVERYDAY, AND DISUSED REALITY OF THE WORLD WE HAD MADE.

He made you see and wonder at that which you would usually ignore. Working in the period when artists had begun to turn old industrial buildings into lofts where they not only worked, but also lived, he became part of a reevaluation and even celebration of the products of the industrial revolution now not as necessary elements of pro-duction—factory halls that made the making of things possible in an efficient manner—but as consumable elements with character, whose textures and expressive pieces could attract memories and associations.

> Not just factories, but warehouses and other anonymous buildings could have a beauty, Gehry and others showed us. Their very plainness, their matter-of-a-fact construction, and their scale had a power that shone out in contrast to the overworked and fussy qualities of most contemporary construction.

What bore the marks of making was and is, ironically perhaps, the most desirable object of consumption. We want authenticity and evidence of our human ability to craft. We also want spaces that are open and abstract enough that we can invent our uses and interpretations. Those car barns in Los Angeles had all those qualities, all the more because they were so outside of everyday use. They reminded us of what was, without any of the treacle of nostalgia that comes out of the renovation of more genteel structures.

Just as important as what Gehry didn't do was what he did: he translated the building and safety codes that define so much of how our buildings look into forms that were no more than what were necessary. The resulting composition of planes, which came not from classical proportions but from negotiations about use fixed in the fat books assembled by building departments, had a beauty that paralleled that of the original buildings, whose forms also came out of both building practices and the need for efficiency and safety.

Architecture could derive its ability to give pleasure from a very different source from what we learn in the history books. Beauty could come organically from the way buildings are made and used.

Frank Gehry's calculated but sincere forthrightness and even matter-of-fact attitude were the final touch that sucked me into this parallel universe where ugly and old were beautiful and new. Sometimes it is indeed a gift to be simple and plain, even if it takes a lot of work to get there.

WHY BEING A GOOD ARCHITECT IS EXPENSIVE

4 Years later, when I was working for Frank Gehry as a junior designer, I found it takes more than skill to be that pure. In that period, a

commission for just one house kept the office going and fed the practice and thus us designers. One of the open secrets of the design profession is that many smaller offices (and even larger ones) survive by doing residential work for very wealthy clients, which subsidizes the designs they do for smaller commercial and less wealthy customers, let alone community or non-profit clients. I knew one firm in San Francisco that produced the most outrageous high-tech designs, all made possible by a decade's worth of work on a very traditional house in Silicon Valley.

There are several reasons for this. Getting a commission for a commercial building is often a very competitive process, with clients being more interested in the bottom line than in the strength of the creativity the architect displays. Poorer clients and non-profit organizations also have less money to spare, but they might let you experiment more. Governments, large institutions, and large commercial clients often set very low fees in advance, even if they give you a chance to create a public monument.

Somebody who wants an architect to design a house and has the means to fulfill a vision of what their home should be chooses an architect based on getting the design that pleases them most, or one that they think will best suit the way they lead their lives. They pay more for a car with bells and whistles, and for clothes that are high design; they expect to do the same for the design of their home.

The architecture of a home is also more complex and therefore costs more (billable) time to design. If you are designing an office building, one floor will tend to be much like the next; in a home, the master bedroom will be different from one of the children's bedrooms, the kitchen different from the living room, and the side that has a view different from the side that faces the neighbors. Moreover, when you are having somebody design your bedroom, you care about the size of the closets, where the doors and windows are, and maybe even what material is used for the handle that lets you open those apertures. The architect has to design all of that. That takes time and thus costs money.

Finally, in the design of a large and complex home, the client and owner often develop a strange and intimate relationship with "their" architect. As the designers wind up knowing intimate details about the clients' lives, they become something between friends and servants, confidants and shrinks. An architect once told me that the number one reason people hire an architect is that they are having marital problems. The process of figuring out how you are going to live, where your bed and your lavatory are going to be, and how large the closets need to be either brings people together into a shared vision (birthed by the architect) or causes a divorce when they realize that they were looking at the world in a different manner. In my own meager experience of trying be an architect, one of my three clients got divorced during the process.

In that kind of a convoluted though often close relationship, it is often difficult for the clients to say no to the architect when she or he proposes changes that are going to drive up the cost. Once the architect has sketched out a vision and seduced the client, there is often no going back.

Finally, the client always realizes they want more. They need more living space, more bedrooms, a fancier bathroom and kitchen, more views, and more gadgets. All of that can cause house designs to go on for years. In the case of the house in Frank Gehry's office, I think it took eight years from the first client meeting until the house was finished. In the meantime, what was already a large house on four lots in Malibu grew to be much larger and also much more elaborate. It was not nearly as expressive as some of Gehry's other work—local regulations and restrictions would not allow that—but the spaces were thought through in large-scale models and countless drawings to make sure that they were as spectacular as possible.

As the house grew in size and complexity, its budget also expanded. It had started at about $1.5 million (or so I was told when I arrived) and had more than doubled by the time I, like nearly everybody in the office, put my time in on its design. Several people in the office did nothing else but work on the house and were thus in effect full-time employees of the client. The cost kept rising. One day, I was waiting outside of Gehry's office to talk to him about another project. He was meeting with the client to tell him that the cost had doubled again. After he had explained the situation, there was short silence in the room, and then I heard the client say: "Well, I guess if you're buying a Picasso, you pay for a Picasso."

Not many architects can command Picasso prices or withstand a comparison to his work, and Gehry was then not nearly as famous as he is today. Yet this client was hooked, and he kept paying until the house was finished. Several years later, he sold it. But, at least for a while, he got to live in a Picasso.

HOW A GOOD ARCHITECT GETS THINGS BUILT

5 What is a good architect? I tried to be one. I worked for another firm for a short while, and then started trying to obtain my own clients. I designed office interiors, a restaurant, and several houses and house remodels. None of them was ever built. I entered competitions. I lost.

Am I a bad architect? Of course not. I am one of the most brilliant architects who has never built, although I have a lot of company. But being an architect who actually gets things built takes a particular combination of talents. Sometimes, as in the case of James Gamble Rogers or a few well-known practitioners today, you don't even really to do much drawing. What you need is a sharp eye, a clear and quick understanding of what works and what is good, the ability to sell the design and seduce the client, the skill to run the office, and the stamina to work with construction people and building departments to see the project through to opening day. You can delegate most of that work, but you have to know how to lead the effort.

I think I have a good eye, a talent to put forms together and shape spaces, and the ability to sell the whole package (are you buying this?).

Yet there is something else you have to be able to do.

YOU HAVE TO BE ABLE TO CONVINCE YOURSELF AND YOUR CLIENT THAT WHAT YOU ARE DESIGNING IS MEANT TO BE.

You have to have the conviction and the verve in drawing and presentation to make your design seem like destiny.

I do not have that ability. But I have been in many situations where I get to see architects who do, and I have made something of a study of their techniques, their tricks, and, at times, their most telling failures.

HOW TO WIN
A COMPETITION

6 Come in, shake everybody's hands. If you know one of the jury members, ask after their family or their affairs. Go to the front of the room, introduce yourself and make small talk while your assistant prepares the presentation. Start by saying how excited you are by the possibility of this commission, what wonderful challenges it offers, and how you are completely primed for this situation so that you will give it your very best. You will not, of course, even look at any other commissions until this one is done, on time, and on budget, like all your other work.

That is the ritual beginning of just about every selection committee presentation I have attended, whether as part of a candidate team or, as has happened much more often, one of the jurors. It gets to the point that you feel as if you have heard all the jokes before. What is more annoying is to watch certain architects who are not that good as designers, but who are charismatic and charming, seduce the members of the jury who are not professionals. It is not necessarily a male–female act, although the most common set-up in our sexist society is still that most of the architects are men and the non-professional members of the selection committee, especially of cultural institutions, are the wealthy wives of patrons (I'm sorry, but that is the situation). A successful male architect can seduce another male with shared interests in sports or other "manly" pursuits.

The whole system of selecting architects through such processes is problematic for these and many other reasons, but I would argue it is still better than the alternatives. The standard process involves either an open call for qualifications or an expert advisor (a role I have fulfilled a few times) suggesting a list of potential designers; then a discussion around portfolios that whittles the group down to a list of anywhere from five to ten architects whom the committee decides make work that best reflects how they see themselves and their new building; and then interviews during which the finalists will, whether you ask them to or not, invariably present sketch designs. This routine gives you the most options and the best chance to figure out whether an architect might fit your needs.

It is an expensive and time-consuming way to find an architect, and therefore one that is usually only possible when you are selecting an architect for a major cultural, library, university, sports, or governmental building. By its very nature, it reinforces the notion that the issues at hand, whether they are the need for more space or the desire for a new or better identity, can be solved only by building a new structure designed by an architect. In reality, that decision has already been made before the selection starts.

For a juror, there are advantages. It is a luxury to have some of the best architects in the world present their work to you, be able to compare them, and then get down to a small group that you think might do just the right building for the given client and site. It is also, truth be told, fun to watch architects performing, but they will all lose by doing this: making a design in the last round of selection such as this can cost up to half a million dollars, and often at least $100,000. Even if the client has a budget to pay for designs, the architects' costs will be many times what they are given.

When I was working for Frank Gehry, I convinced him to let me enter a competition that he felt we were bound to lose. The office would receive a small amount of money to enter, and I assured Gehry that we would do it in a low-key manner. At first, only an intern and I would work on the competition, consulting with him and the other senior designers as necessary. Only in the last three weeks would we make a core design group of half a dozen people, and in the last few days we would be able to rely on the rest of the office to make the presentation drawings and models that I felt would help us win the competition.

All went well until the final few days, when the competition quickly sucked up the whole office in a frenetic push to make the best possible design and show it most beautifully. The afternoon the project had to be shipped out via FedEx was complete mayhem, culminating with Gehry standing over the model, already in its crate, making changes before the lid went on while one of the receptionists distracted the FedEx pick-up guy waiting by the door. We closed the crate, sent it off, and I commented to Berta Gehry, Frank's wife and office manager, that I had kept my promise not to go over budget. She just arched her eyebrow and said: "We'll see." I went to have a drink, and then went to sleep for the first time in several days.

When I came back to my desk to clean up and move onto the next project, Berta walked past and casually dropped the receipts and time sheets for the competition in front of me. She didn't say anything, but we had spent over $150,000 on a project that we indeed did not win.

Almost a decade later, I was advising the Cincinnati Contemporary Arts Center as it selected the architect for a new building. Its director, Charles Desmarais, believed that art at the end of the 20th century was changing in ways that would make the traditional white-walled gallery obsolete. He wanted an architect and a design that would redefine the relationship between art, architecture, and the city. As a result, the final list of candidates was unusual in that it focused on architects who were then thought of as radical, untested, and even not really architects: they included Zaha Hadid, Rem Koolhaas, Bernard Tschumi, Diller and Scofidio, and Daniel Libeskind.

Each architect came in and made their presentation. Several of them were less practiced in the niceties of handling especially wealthy donors, but most made a valiant effort. We were waiting for Rem Koolhaas to appear when I excused myself to go to the bathroom. I passed him outside, pacing back and forth. Though we knew each other, he barely acknowledged my existence. I went back into the room, we called in Koolhaas, and he stormed in without greeting anybody. He immediately started talking about his proposal while pointing to various aspects of his—brilliant and appropriate for this commission—previous designs, all the while keeping his back turned to his audience.

I do not remember what his design was. All I recall is the looks the jury members shot each other and me. They could never imagine working with this man. And all I could think about was all the money and all the hours he and his office had spent coming up with what was no doubt a fascinating design, one that none of us would really take seriously.

HOW GOOD WORK WILL OUT

7 People often complain about the "star system" in architecture. THEY BELIEVE THAT THERE IS SOME MYSTERIOUS CONSPIR-ACY THAT TURNS WORTHLESS DESIGNERS INTO SUPERSTARS WHILE IGNORING THE IMPORTANT WORK OF MUCH BETTER DESIGNERS. Some architects believe this too: it wasn't until the British architect David Chipperfield was knighted and snarfed up half the museum commissions on the planet that he stopped complaining about less worthy architects stealing all the work with their flashy designs while solid, thoughtful people such as himself were excluded by the conspiracy of critics and clients.

Chipperfield has made some good buildings, but also quite a few mediocre ones. His entry in a competition I helped to judge in Mexico City in 2004 reminded me of that and illustrated the fact that there is no such conspiracy, but that the notion of such a cabal is a ready excuse when good work wins out.

Sometimes it is very difficult to decide the best project in a competition, and sometimes it is not. The latter was the case in the competition for the Biblioteca Vasconcelos in Mexico City. The project was a vanity endeavor for the then-president of the country, who wanted a publicly accessible library (as opposed to the academic and expert institutions that made it difficult for most people to use them) in a run-down neighborhood that was home to an outdoor market. The building had to open before the president's term ended, which unfortunately meant that the built result was compromised by hasty construction and cost cutting.

After the jury had reviewed the finalists, each of whom had made a full design for the project, it was immediately clear to almost all of us that one of the candidates had created a design whose originality and clarity made it stand apart from the other competitors. We were also pleased that, even though this was an international competition, which was rare for Mexico, the designer, Alberto Kalach, was a local architect who had made some beautiful buildings already. He was obviously up to the task.

Kalach's design consisted of one space in which the stacks would hang from the ceiling, leaving the main floor open as a grand reading room. The books would hover over you as you were walking down the aisles, and balconies would intermingle with the stacks so that you could hide in an attic of books. The building would be partially buried in a jungle that would serve as a living library of Mexico's landscape.

There was a precedent for the design: a utopian vision drawn up by Étienne-Louis Boullée in 1785. The fragmentation of that vision of one large, vaulted space with its books arranged in tiers on the sides into an upside-down forest of books through which you would go wandering made the images all the more compelling.

We all agreed that this design had to be the winning one—at least almost all of us. Only one of the jurors demurred, preferring Chipperfield's elegant but rather mundane and, what was more important, monumental and closed scheme that had none of the democratic character Kalach promised.

We were surprised but heard him out and argued for hours, even though he was the only dissenter. Finally, felled by jet lag, he fell asleep during our discussions and, after he awoke, we quickly voted for the Kalach scheme. He was furious, going as far as to vent his frustrations to the Minister of Culture who was managing the project and to voice his dissent in public. That did not prevent the library from being constructed and, although it is still not quite finished after all these years and its shelves not filled, it is one of the most beautiful library spaces I know.

HOW DREAMS DIE IN THE PROCESS

8 Even if you win a commission, it does not mean that you will see the opening day. The larger and more complex the project, or the more daring the design, the less likely it is that it will ever be built. For hundreds of years, architects have dreamed of building the best possible place, one that is more than just one building, becoming a city where all is absolutely right. Renaissance painters envisioned structures arrayed in perfect grids, writers spoke of utopia, and architects—including Boullée—imagined perfect worlds of spheres that offered a respite from the messy realities of everyday life. Few such places are ever built, and whenever some place comes close, like the new capital that the Brazilians hewed out of the inland forests and called Brasilia, or the smaller communes that have sprung up over the years, they never live up to their ideals. Sometimes I wonder whether the best designs are unbuilt by definition:

THE BETTER THE ARCHITECTURE AS A PROPOSAL, THE MORE DIFFICULT IT IS TO LIVE UP TO ITS VISION ONCE YOU HAVE TO MAKE IT REAL.

A few years ago, I was part of a supervisory committee that oversaw the development of a new city that is being constructed outside of Moscow. Called Skolkovo, it was the brainchild of former Russian President Dmitry Medvedev, who apparently visited Silicon Valley and decided that his country needed something like that.

The committee included both Russian experts and architects and advisors from around the world. The first thing we had to do was to choose a master plan. Though the proposal that was most idealistic and ambitious came from the Office for Metropolitan Architecture, OMA (though without Rem Koolhaas), the Russians thought it was too nostalgic for that other time when they had tried to build utopias under a communist realm. So we picked another scheme, one that was much more mundane. What made it idealistic was not only that we were going to choose the world's best architects to design the buildings there, but that it would be a car-free, carbon-neutral place filled with parks, playgrounds, places of culture and collaboration, and clusters of houses that would be open to nature.

It did not come to nothing, but what is finally being built is of much less interest. The cars are back, the parks are smaller, the buildings are on the whole very conventional, and the large cultural institutions are vestigial. Only a small tower that will contain Medvedev's think tank and apartment remains as reminder of the ideals of what is now essentially just another research and development park.

> What ultimately killed the dream was a combination of unrealistic expectations and political realities. After Putin, Medvedev's predecessor and successor, took power, state interest shifted to other areas. As the project developed, bean counters and potential users began to carry most of the arguments. Eventually they got rid of the troublesome committee and just ran Skolkovo as a regular development.

The emblems for the plan's ambitions and utopian ideals were two proposals of a vast scale and uncertain function. OMA, which was given a commission for a central, multi-use structure as a consolation prize for not winning the right to do the whole of Skolkovo, proposed a forty-story cube standing on one point. It would have been a daring symbol of what architecture could do, both structurally and in terms of image: defying gravity, perfect as a piece of geometry, huge in scale, and mixing a host of different functions together.

> The Japanese architect Kazuyo Sejima proposed a softer but even larger structure: a dome almost fifty stories tall covering a landscape that would be lush and livable even in the middle of the Russian winter. It would be so large that it would create its own weather, with clouds forming in the glass and steel's upper structure.

Together, these designs represented the most extreme ambitions in architecture: to create an ideal shape that removed itself from our everyday experience and created a new world; and an Eden-like place where all forms would dissolve and a new nature would take over. They stood in a long line of architecture trying to be as big and perfect as possible. Together, they would have cost over $1 billion.

The Skolkovo administration asked for modification, for something less ideal. The architects were not interested. Like most grand schemes, they remain as visions of what could have been.

HOW PERFECTION KILLS

9 The ideas that architecture should both build an ideal structure and should lead us back to Eden are engrained in the discipline. They haunt every form, every project, and every proposal. They lurk behind even the most modest scheme by an architecture student. We cannot escape the notion that we need to make the perfect form, space, and image, while we also want to return, maybe in that same effort, to something before human-made forms, spaces, and images.

Where did this utopian ghost come from? Why does it haunt us to this day?

It all starts with the beginning, or at least what architects imagine that to be. There are many myths about how architecture started and what its basic elements might be. The most popular and enduring of them was articulated most clearly by the French Abbé Laugier in 1753 in his *Essai sur l'Architecture*. For Laugier, it all began with the making of a basic temple shape. Man (not woman) wanted shelter from storms and the sun, and created it by planting four tree posts in the ground to act as vertical supports, connecting them at the top with beams, and then laying a thatched roof on top of that.

This seems fairly straightforward, but Laugier elaborated on his theory by seeing in the wooden posts nascent columns, in the beam an entablature, and in the roof the triangular temple front. The whole building became not just a house, but really a temple —a place for gods, not men, to live.

What lurks behind this jump is the fact that, to most critics and historians of architecture from the Renaissance through the 19th century, real architecture did not start with such a "primitive hut," but with Greek classical architecture. This architecture was, according to Laugier and others, a translation of wood construction into stone to make it more solid and durable. The three classical orders reflected the different character architecture could take. The Doric is both more masculine and more primitive, and thus fundamental. The Ionic is more feminine and gracious. The Corinthian, finally, is the most ornate and complex, and perhaps also a bit decadent.

Everything that has happened in architecture since then is just a development, translation, and elaboration of those orders of columns, becoming a system of plinths, entablatures, and pediments, and then the subsidiary parts of a temple, such as architraves, metopes, and triglyphs, and then into the building blocks for structures that were not necessarily places for gods and goddesses, but of importance nonetheless. Palaces and meeting houses, and later museums, theaters, banks, and any other monuments to wealth and power, were to be essentially temples.

For that reason, architecture became about death and dead things, or, to put it in a less leaden manner, about eternal values. Architecture housed entities that lived forever. They should also last for eternity.

Later, it was a storeroom—literally, in the case of one of the more perfect classical buildings, the Athenian Treasury in Delphi, or, figuratively, the kind of massive structures that architects built out of stone—to encase the values (and, in the example of banks, the value) of the people who commissioned the structure.

Behind the temple lay those structures for which you can make an even better case as being the first works of true architecture, namely the grave monuments many cultures began erecting for their leaders when they had accumulated enough wealth to do so. The largest and most famous of these are the Egyptian pyramids, but from Asia to South America you can find the remains of giant structures that had at their core just one chamber, the burial place of the ruler. These structures were death embodied in both form and appearance.

You could argue that they were also about another life, whether the realm of the gods or that of the afterlife, but that only emphasizes what they are not about: the reality of human life, encased in a body, subject to joys and suffering, and finite in its duration. The only true architecture, Adolf Loos once said, is a gravestone you come across in the middle of a forest.

It has always been strange to me that architecture roots itself so much in death and looks forward so much to something that is not human. From these origin myths comes the idea that architecture should be made of perfect pieces, should be larger and more abstract than our daily lives, and should stand for something we can never achieve in this life. This architecture is by its very nature alien.

To this day, we associate good architecture with something that is big, permanent, and abstract. This tradition was formalized at the school that defined the discipline for almost three centuries, from the middle of the 17th century until the beginning of the 20th: the École des Beaux-Arts in Paris. There you learned that there were basic and unchanging rules that had shaped those temples and should shape your designs. They were based both in mathematics and in the structural reality of stone construction. Any building was an elaboration of grids and hierarchical layouts that you could trace back to temple designs. Architecture concerned itself only with the central buildings of the state. Anything else, from the houses of the mere middle class to stores, let alone such new structures as train stations or department stores, was the realm of builders.

Though architecture has opened up since then, its roots and its prejudices are still the result of these dogmas. We focus on monumental structures, whether they are museums or opera houses, and love those columns turned into structures of an inhuman scale we call skyscrapers. What is just as important is that we (that is, architecture junkies and designers) value the abstraction and regularity of buildings, as well as their permanence. Any sign of imperfection or of human use, any mark the weather makes on a building, is a defect.

WHY ARCHITECTURE DOESN'T MATTER– IN OUR DAILY LIFE

10 There is a beauty to monumental architecture that anyone, whether an architect or not, can see. Buildings that are big and well organized impress us with size and clarity. A well-proportioned façade and an intricate floor plan are things of beauty as well, drawing us through a structure, but also revealing the building, in the abstraction of a drawing, as an artifact that gains power from its rhythms and grids. Then reality intrudes: the weather and wear and tear take away from the monument's perfection, and, horror of horrors, actual users show up. When you take a photograph, you make sure the weather stripping doesn't show and there are no people anywhere to be seen.

But this monumental architecture exists largely outside of our daily life. As it is reserved for big, important buildings, and not for our houses or our daily places of work or play, we think of it as special, which also means that it is not really comfortable. When architects do design homes, they are either the rambling palaces of rich people or the blocks in which we can rent a few square meters, and which are generic and often quite restrictive. In either case, we as users then come in and decorate the spaces, making them more sensitive and sensible, more fitting to our lives.

The situation is even worse at work, where we find ourselves locked into Dilbertland or vying for the largest office. There, architecture recedes into the grid of columns or the monumental entrance hall where we are meant to be impressed by the company or agency we are entering.

Most restaurants and bars are created by interior designers (if there is an architect at all), who figure out how to make a comfortable interior. The architecture recedes in dim light or behind screens. Only the large places of public and communal recreation, such as concert halls or sports arenas, reveal architecture, whether it is in the stretch of the girders and trusses that show us the order that makes these large spaces, in the grids of columns that organize our viewing in space, or in the sweep of lobbies that make us feel small. Everywhere we are the passive consumers of something larger and other than us.

> The basic elements and the origin history of architecture make designers create alien and large things that elevate and entomb us in memorials to unchangeable facts and abstract ideas. The very embodiment of human ideals, they are a-human.

THE RESULT OF THIS OBSESSION WITH MONUMENTALITY IS THAT ARCHITECTURE EXISTS LARGELY OUTSIDE OF OUR DAILY LIFE.

WHY IT IS BETTER TO GATHER THAN TO ERECT

11 There is another history of architecture. It is one that was noted by 19th-century critics such as Eugène-Étienne Viollet-le-Duc and Gottfried Semper, but somehow has never become the mainstream story architects tell themselves. It starts with people gathering around a fire, decorating a cave, and weaving together shelters. It starts with making something that already exists into a place that is comfortable for humans and decorating it to represent the world to ourselves. It starts with sociality and centeredness.

It starts as an extension of your clothing into something that contains more than just you and represents more than just you. Architecture in this version comes from the need to be together in a place. It frames a relationship with others that you recognize as human beings in relation to nature. By creating a place, whether in the cave or around the fire, or on the steppes in a tent, it marks the space where you are, with others, while you orient yourself by the rocks or the trees or the distant vistas.

WHERE ARCHITECTURE IS, YOU ARE HOME.

Architecture here is not the result of destroying nature, of cutting things down and shaping them into something they are not, but of gathering together what nature offers, whether it is twigs and leaves or, later, mud to make bricks. Architecture starts as marking place, and then proceeds from there to elaborate that place and what it consists of into form. It is the weaving together of disparate pieces to create shelter, or the molding and stacking of fluid materials into something solid and enclosing.

As humans make these shelters, patterns appear. They are not applied or extraneous, as is ornament on temples, but rather they come out of the order of the materials themselves, leading to geometries and layers of colors that are more complex. Instead of structural hierarchy, the desire to make a fitting enclosure leads forms to stretch, bend, curve, expand, and contract. Rhythms appear out of materials and use.

The problem of such structures, but also their beauty, is that they do not last very long. If you weave together a tent or shelter out of branches and leaves, you will either leave it behind as you move on, or you will keep adding to it and changing it. A tent that you make out of hides and sticks is something that appears and disappears whenever you camp. Decorations fade or you paint them over. The work is truly organic, and goes back to nature. It lasts as long as your need for it or your commitment to it.

> A few years ago, the designer Jurgen Bey created a proposal for a bench in Germany. He noticed that, every fall, armies of gardeners raked up all the fallen leaves, gathered them together, and then composted or burned them. Instead, he designed an attachment to the trailer and cart that went around the park picking up the leaves. A small motor would push the leaves into the attachment, which he had shaped so that, as they became compacted, they would take on the form of a bench, which would slide out the tractor's rear end along the path. You could then sit on the bench for as long as it lasted, before wind and rain made it dissolve back into the ground.

We have much less poetic versions of such structures everywhere today. They are called pop-ups: often containers, they are sometimes just bits of canvas and scaffolding, and house stores or restaurants during a festival or whenever and wherever a lot of people gather. They are utilitarian, but full of life and often ingenious in their designs. Few architects ever design them.

> We also have more serious temporary shelters: refugee camps. The problem of transitory populations, driven out of their homes by war, famine, or natural disasters, has taken on epic proportions. Yet few designers take the problem seriously—because, if the camps work, they will disappear. They are not monuments. They will not offer either a good fee or a lasting memorial to either the designer's or the client's achievements. This is where architecture needs to focus and find a way to use its other traditions to offer a real contribution to our society.

WHY IT ALL
HAPPENS IN CHINA

12 Nowhere does the future of architecture matter more than in China, where a building boom is under way that is by now legendary in its ability to add huge amounts of dwellings and office buildings, not to mention the infrastructure that ties together the new insta-cities and the civic monuments that the authorities believe will make them into important places.

Most of the focus has been on creating as many little boxes as fast as possible. Beyond that, there has been a desire to create structures that catch the eye and represent the wealth and sophistication of these cities. Yet, just as everything else is happening more quickly in China, so also the realization that the traditional focus the country adopted from the West might not be the best way to build truly livable environments. Even as the first boom was happening, back in the 1990s, artists and architects were carving out spaces to live, work, and play that reused old factories and even apartment buildings. Some of these "relics" are as young as twenty years old. There is also a fascination with building things that are temporary, eschewing the focus on grand and static monuments meant to last for ages that is so central to Western architecture; coming from a culture that has long rebuilt its structures continually, China seems to be moving toward a new realization of what architecture can be at an accelerated rate.

In 2015, I co-curated the Shenzhen and Hong Kong Bi-City Biennale of Urbanism and Architecture. Working with the architects

Alfredo Brillembourg, Hubert Klumpner, and Doreen Liu, I tried to make an exhibition that would show how we could gather together the forms and buildings that already exist to reinvigorate, open up, or just jazz up our existing homes, offices, streets, and even whole cities. My fellow curators did so on the larger scale of those cities, collecting proposals that would combine "top-down" planning, in which politicians, bureaucrats, and designers lay down their vision of what our cities should be in the future, and developers then fill them in with boxes that are as efficient and saleable as possible, with "bottom-up" action in which ordinary people take charge of their own spaces.

I decided to concentrate on the smaller scale of how designers can take the materials and spaces of everyday life and transform them through design. What that transformation might be for, I left to the designers. All I asked was that they indicate some sort of scenario that might allow the inhabitants of a city that is growing at an insane pace (it was a fishing village of less than 20,000 people in the 1970s, and is now a metropolis of over 10 million) to make better use of the often inadequate space they have in which to live, play, work, and gather.

The result was a collection of installations that varied from the whimsical (Carlos Jiménez's installation of toys made in Shenzhen that he bought in LA, brought back home and placed in a kind of abstract dollhouse) to the hardheaded (a room made out of reused beer cartons, designed by Feng Feng, that he rented out on Airbnb). My favorite, though, was an installation by the architect Francesco Delogu, an old friend I had called in at the last moment when one of the other participants dropped out, and the artist Maria Cristina Finucci. They in turn enlisted the help of two young architects, Giovanni Vimercati and David Tantimonaco, who spent several weeks in Shenzhen trolling the streets for cast-offs, cheap gizmos and gadgets, and just plain refuse.

They assembled all this into walls of plastic cartons they arranged to enclose a small room, hung with a single light bulb, and extended to shield the other installations from a large garage door that opened up from the exhibition space to the outside. Crammed full of objects of many colors and forms, these walls became a tapestry that held your eye with the sheer variety of visual information. As you looked closer, you could make out the individual bits and pieces and marvel at the shape of a doll's arm, a piece of chair, a sex toy (how did that get in there?), or torn-out bits of a magazine. Removed from their original form, they took on a life and beauty all their own. Instead of wondering what they were for, you started to look at what they were, both as bits by themselves and as part of the larger patterns to which they contributed.

Delogu and Finucci, in other words, had found order in disorder and meaning in leftovers. To drive that point home, they lined the inside of the room formed by the intersection of the walls with secondhand or discarded books. They placed those books with their spines facing in, so all you could see was the ends of the pages. You could not gain information—the books were not doing their job—but their mass created a stillness where you could reflect on the fullness around you while you took in the odor of the paper. Nostalgia and a sense of loss balanced the onslaught of forms and colors all around you. Here was an architecture that was not monumental, but that gathered the place around you and turned it into a cocoon you could, if even for a moment, inhabit and understand.

HOW TO SHOW
WHAT IS ALREADY
THERE

13 The name for this kind of work is "bricolage." It means the gathering together of disparate bits and pieces into something that is not a whole but has coherence. There is a long tradition of self-taught artists and architects working in this way. In the United States, the most famous example of a bricolage is the Watts Tower, a rank of spires the handyman Simon Rodia put together between 1921 and 1954 in Los Angeles. Bits and pieces of tile line concrete and masonry walls out of which the twisting towers rise with no particular purpose other than to mark the place and, perhaps, offer a lasting autobiography, a sort of enigmatic monument, of Rodia.

The ethnographer and philosopher Claude Lévi-Strauss argued in *The Savage Mind*, a seminal book first published in France in 1962 and based on his research in the Amazon, that bricolage was not just evidence of a lack of training or purpose, but an alternative to the ways of logic and "science." Scientists, Lévi-Strauss stated, start with an observation of real things, then subject them to organization and analysis, finally to derive classifications and conclusions that are abstract. Bricoleurs, he said, do the opposite. They arrange, assemble, and connect objects they find all around them, allowing an order to come out of the relationships that these things have as objects you can see, feel, or taste. The assembly is the point: in the manner in which things are assembled, balance or tension appears that realigns the forces of the universe through the relationship between concrete things. In this way, unseen forces become evident and play themselves out in the stuff all around you.

What is important from Lévi-Strauss's perspective is that the leaves, seeds, bits of bark, or shells and rocks are not removed from the world of which they are part, nor are they just evidence of something. Rather, their very nature as things becomes evident and is intensified, perhaps even crystalized, by their assembly. THE MAGIC OF DESIGN IS TO BRING OUT THAT WHICH IS THERE, BUT WHICH WE DO NOT ALWAYS SEE. The beauty of things shines forth through the act of the bricoleur.

It makes us realize how little we value what is all around us. That is because most of what we see is of a make-up and kind that are difficult to define. Most of the materials, forms, and images we encounter are artificial. Our walls are made out of concrete, which is a combination of ground-up rocks, sand, and chemicals. They are covered with plaster or paint, which is more morcellated material. Our structures can also be steel, which is the result of melting ores and, again, adding chemicals. Our windows are made out of glass —more melting and mixing, which we also use to make bricks. Even such natural materials as wood or stone present themselves to us in fragments that we have cut, polished, and otherwise turned into something they were not when we first found them in nature.

In reaction, some architects have made a fetish of "real" materials. They try to bring back "craftsmanship" and reveal connections between two pieces of wood. They torture stone and even concrete to show us how it was made, leaving the holes where the pieces of wood were held together in the finished plane, along with the texture of that wood and the ragged edges where the formwork ended, as if that would give us a sense of the reality of this human-made material. It does, but only in a manner that makes us realize how far we remove from its original state everything with which we surround ourselves.

All that work, by the way, involves a huge amount of energy, almost all of which is wasted in the process. To smelt and shape steel, to mix concrete, and even to cut wood uses up vast amounts of natural resources. Using natural materials only cuts down on that waste a little bit.

What if we were to act as bricoleurs, and gather together existing materials and forms, and give them meaning, beauty, and use by reassembling them?

WHY IT IS IMPORTANT TO GO SLUMMING

14 What makes bricolage important is not just that it is a way of making that breaks through hierarchies and doesn't worry about perfection, focusing instead on how we make ourselves recognizable and at home in the world. Bricolage also matters because it is the art of poverty rather than of surplus. It is what you make with what is around you, and for millions of people around the globe that is the only way they can create architecture. We just don't call it architecture, because we think of it as shelter for people in poverty and, because it comes out of deprivation, we think of it as something low and not worth considering. Even worse, if we do take bricolage seriously, we run the danger of, quite literally, slumming.

Several years ago, I found myself in Mumbai and was invited to go on a tour of the largest slum in the city, Dharavi. It is home to over a million people, who live in the worst kind of poverty, in conditions that are horrific. The first thing that I saw when I walked in there was a dog whose pinkish skin, reflecting the polluted water he drank, barely clung to his skeleton. The dirt, smells, and signs of malnutrition were overwhelming.

But so was the beauty and industry the place evidences. I was told that Dharavi produced over a billion dollars' worth of economic value every year, and I was not surprised. What is even more remarkable is that almost all of the economy is based on recycling. The very place consists of shacks the inhabitants have made out of scraps of metal, wood, plastic sheeting, or whatever else they could find around. Some of the houses and shops are quite elaborate, and the whole neighborhood is dotted with squares where people can gather, and where kids play games using balls and posts they have improvised. Yes, it is a slum, but one with an incredible texture and complexity that leads you on from house to house and street to street.

The floor of one of the first workshops I saw was piled with boxes. Men slept on some of them, while others sorted them into stacks that made little sense to me. Then they put them into an antiquated set of machines, apparently salvaged from Eastern Europe, and at the other end brand new boxes came out. So it was in every place we visited: a structure salvaged from the remains of a consumer-oriented society, whose textures, shapes, and colors echoed with memories of their former use, assembled into a tense and fragile cohesion to house not only people, but the act of continually remaking that world in such a way that it kept the community going.

The question is whether we can learn lessons from Dharavi while also helping that community become a healthier place to live, with the facilities that will help its young have opportunities beyond this slum. Can we separate the beauty, the industry, and the cohesion of Dharavi from the abject poverty and misery that pervade this city-within-a-city?

High-rises are going up all around Dharavi, and the government would love to see the slum go away completely. It would be more logical to tear down these shacks, put in sewage and water lines, and provide social housing that would be efficient and reasonably safe and sound. It would also destroy what makes Dharavi so amazing.

The other thing that makes this a difficult lesson to learn is that we associate bricolage with "primitive" cultures (as Lévi-Strauss himself called the tribes where he observed bricolage) and with poverty in our own society. Our whole society is focused on the latest, the newest, the shiniest, and the most perfect, from our bodies to our buildings to our cars and household objects. What we need more than anything else, in architecture and in much else, is to find a way to value reuse, reimagination, and recycling.

HOW TO DESIGN
WITH DRY HUMOR

15 These days, the reuse and particularly the repurposing of found and used materials are almost acceptable and even chic, and that is largely because of the influence of a small group of designers who transformed a movement with roots in the squatter movement and hippie-dom into high design.

In 1992, a small exhibit in Milan astonished the design world. Every year in the spring, thousands of designers, manufacturers, and design aficionados descend on this otherwise rather drab city for the Salone del Mobile, the annual furniture fair. It is a huge event if you are in the sofa business, but over the years it has also begun to attract those interested in the industry's fringes. Small exhibitions showcase designs that might not be so comfortable or even make-able, but that test ideas about what comfort or just the idea of sitting might mean. Lectures and workshops and, what is most important, parties spill out into the streets, turning whole parts of the city into a movable feast marked by the high design not only of the objects discussed or displayed, but also the ones worn by the crowd.

In this particular year, a group of Dutch designers and critics has banded together to show some of their experiments. They called themselves Droog, which means "dry" in Dutch. It was a nonsense name, but one with overtones of dry wit and neutral, no-nonsense design. What they showed was a chandelier made out of eighty-five bare light bulbs cinched together; furniture made out of scraps the designer had found at the flea market; ceramics that combined found fragments with new clay; and chairs that looked like a kid's drawing. There were no whiplash curves teased out of bent wood or carved out of marble, no decorations unless they had been part of whatever the designers found, and no pretension other than to question what a piece of furniture actually was and how it should be made.

The collection exploded preconceptions and made design stars out of half a dozen of its participants. Over the years, Droog has gone on to become an established brand, and its co-creator and director, Renny Ramakers, is less interested in reuse and bricolage than in larger social issues. But the reverberations of those early collections have been felt all around the world, so that now furniture made out of recycled material is not shabby but chic. Droog showed that good design could mean reimaging the forms we already have and reusing materials.

In time, some of the Droog designers, such as Marcel Wanders and Piet Hein Eek, have moved into architecture, creating interiors and even whole buildings. But they have also influenced several generations of architects who have picked up on their techniques and attitudes. One of the most interesting of these is a firm that called itself 2012 Architecten and now goes by the name Superuse Studio. They tied the notion of reuse to the spread of digital technology and mapping in their "Harvest Maps," which started as a documentation of their own search for materials that they could use in their projects. They went beyond the usual cast-off lumber—which by now has become quite mainstream because it provides that instantly weathered, "distressed" look so popular among quasi-urban pioneers—to find ways in which they could use discarded washing machines and kitchen sinks. They turned tire trucks into sofas and car seats into seating for a small theater.

What is just as important is that they made their Harvest Maps available as open-source software that anybody can use to locate materials in their home area. Architecture has a well-established supply chain, as well as a long history of translating drawings into built projects by using known materials that have standard dimensions, and a way of planning buildings that envisions the final look and cost (its value in both an economic and aesthetic sense) because the palette is so known. If we are going to do things in a different manner, we need to develop these methods as well.

This movement is still in its infancy. Moreover, the very notion of bricolage precludes much prediction. The method is ad hoc: you find something, it works well in one place, fits well with something, needs a little something else to fill a gap, implies something else that extends the combination you just made, and suggests a space that might be different from what you envisaged when you started with the first piece. You cannot predict what will happen next, though you can have a general idea of what you have in mind. In fact, when Superuse Studio has tried to apply its methodology to more standard situations such as single-family homes, the results have looked awkward, seemed uncomfortable, and been expensive.

Bricolage, in other words, implies rethinking architecture on a fundamental level. Instead of planning buildings or cities, it works when it responds to particular situations, such as a need for space or the abundance of a particular material. It reinvents itself and its form in its making. All around the world, from Rural Studio working in the poorest county in the United States to provide housing and community structures, to the firm Amateur Architecture in China building structures out of recycled bricks, the notion that we should not use up new materials is taking hold.

> The best of such work both builds on much older traditions of renovation and reuse for its discipline, and recognizes a simple fact: because of the ever-increasing efficiency of the building trades, we invest less and less in new buildings, which means that they are cheaply built and have fewer and fewer actual materials, let alone embellishments. That means that the older something is, the better it was usually built and the more stuff there is to work with, from solid walls to detailing that delights. Renovations almost always result in spaces that have more complexity. Because the memories of use and human occupation adhere to the skin of almost everything you touch, they avoid the neutral quality that pervades even the best-designed new space. Any cut or alteration to such an old envelope feels immediately like a radical act that opens up new views, a different perspective, or even a sense of violence that makes you aware of the temporality of all things.

Bricolage and reuse of existing structures together provide the alternative to the mindless production of new buildings that too often disappoint. It also offers a way out for architects who feel trapped in a profession in which they have to serve those clients who have the money and power to hire them, and then find themselves imposing a vision and set of values that is partially their own, and partially that of their clients, on whoever might use or see their buildings. Instead, this kind of approach lets the architect go exploring through communities, finding ways to use their skills and knowledge to transform what is left over into what could be.

HOW TO PICK ARCHITECTURE OFF THE SHELF

16 It was not just in Europe or in Mumbai slums that reuse became a viable strategy. Starting in the early 1990s, some architects thought they could take apart and reconstruct the American home in a way that would make use of modern technology. I called it "Home Depot modernism," after the popular DIY chain that had just sprung up in suburbs all across the country. It is an approach I still think has the potential to make bricolage a more natural part of our building and design process.

We already buy so many of the bits and pieces that make up our environment at such stores, as well as at places such as IKEA. Only very few of us have the luxury of commissioning an architect to design our house, place of work, or place of recreation. And very few of us can afford the expense or time to coordinate those parts of it that we actually see and use every day by employing a professional interior designer. As a result, architecture has to be rather grand and monumental to even become noticeable to us as users.

Instead, what we really know and can control are our furnishings, which we arrange to conform to our body and our social rituals. We clad such surfaces as we can with paint or materials that suit our moods. Everywhere around us we focus on those things we can manipulate to our wishes. In public spaces, good designers work hard to emphasize us and our needs, making us feel and look good while creating an atmosphere that evokes another place—a bar from the 19th century, an old store instead of the shopping mall in which it is placed, or a living room in an airport. Only in the grandest spaces, those reserved for important things and events such as cultural centers, places of worship, or sports stadia, does the architecture really impress itself on us.

Most of what is around us is "soft architecture," as the Spanish architects Langarita-Navarro call it: the pliable and expandable stuff that is in many ways an extension of our clothes or an intensification of the ethereal bubbles we create around ourselves with lights, air conditioning, heating, cell signals, and computer projections. We live in our cocoons, leaving markers of our lives around our office cubicles, the mark of our body on our chairs, and coverings over the harshest bits of technology, from lamps to computers, that surround us.

We like to think that only grand architecture really matters, while what we do within buildings is just for comfort and convenience. We also like to imagine that architecture creates a framework that orders, composes, and gives meaning to what we place within its structures.

That might be, but most of the time it is the furniture and the décor that we experience. So why can't we build up an architecture out of that?

WHAT WE SHOULD REALLY BE LOOKING AT AND WORKING WITH ARE THOSE THINGS THAT ALLOW US TO TRULY BE AT HOME IN THIS MODERN WORLD.

So walk down the aisle of your typical DIY store. You will find not only hardware, but most of the elements you need to create that home. You can find the doors, the curtains, the flooring, the paint, the windows, and the lumber out of which you can build a place to live or work. About the only thing missing is the structure itself, but that is not something you usually see.

Take the bits and pieces you find there and put them together. If you are an architect, you can do so with the skill proper to your discipline. You can also invent uses and connections manufacturers never intended. This is what is interesting about the practitioners of Home Depot modernism. They could use hardware intended for plumbing as lamps or as window frames. They could take clamps that carpenters use to hold pieces of wood in place and make them into permanent connections between different piece of furniture. They could find ways to make sheets of plastic look beautiful as part of the composition of a room.

Even if you have never been trained as an architect, you can do this. That is the point of a bricolage: it relies on intuition rather than science. But, if you do have the skills proper to architecture, you can more readily make your bricolage something that partakes of more complex and larger structures, both literally and figuratively. You can allude to classical orders with pipes, and frame sequences of spaces with pieces of plywood held together with clamps. You can find and make evident the relationship between the shelter the interior provides and the expanse outside.

It can be delightful to walk down the aisles of a DIY store or wander along the paths IKEA sets out for us. We can imagine taking that experience and turning it into architecture. What remains, then, is for architecture to become part of both the human and the natural landscape around it. An architecture that is a bricolage and a reuse of both landscape and material can be a response to sprawl and mountains, and a way to mark and know your place.

HOW TO KEEP THE
PAST PRESENT

17 One of the first times I realized that renovation could be more than just fixing up an old building was when I visited the house that the artist David Ireland had, in the 1970s, transformed into an art project in San Francisco's Mission Street. It was not a particularly grand mansion and had not been particularly well used over the generations, but for Ireland it was a gold mine. Walking into the house was like taking a trip into the lives of many people I will never know, starting with Ireland himself. The hole where a stove had banged into a wall (for the second time) when he was trying to move the heavy object was duly memorialized with a bronze plaque—it reminded me of reverently staring at the bullet hole in the palace in Delft where the Netherlands' founding father, William I, Prince of Orange, was shot and killed by an assassin. Pieces of wallpaper from different periods remained after Ireland's stripping, carefully preserved so that you could read them as maps of past generations' lives in the home.

Household objects the artist had used, then liked because of the way the broom leaned against the stool or the bucket sat on the floor, remained there forever, basking in the light and our views. Almost every surface was covered with shellac or polish, so that each space gleamed and glistened.

Ireland, in other words, had turned the Capp Street House, as it became known, into a three-dimensional snapshot that condensed and fixed time. It was and is a kind of anti-monument that lasts because of the beauty of its humble materials and time-bound subject matter. It also invented history by the way the artist selected what to leave and what to scrap, what to abandon and what to keep using, and what to show and what cover over. It made me realize that space, structures, and materials, the basic building blocks of architecture, are not just things that you make, but things that you find. Architecture usually consists of covering, filling, and making the reality of what you have done fade away in favor of use and comfort, leaving only a glimmer of what is well made to delight you.

NOW I UNDERSTOOD THAT ARCHITECTURE CAN ALSO BE DISCOVERING, LEAVING, OPENING UP, AND PAUSING IN MID-WORK, SO THAT WHAT YOU HAVE MADE REMAINS IN SUSPENSION. WHEN YOU ENTER INTO SUCH ARCHITECTURE, YOU CATCH YOUR BREATH AND NEVER QUITE LET IT OUT.

HOW TO SEE ARCHITECTURE BEYOND BUILDINGS

18 To be mindful of what exists and to reuse it does not mean drowning in the everyday. The whole point of good design (and art) is that it makes us look, see, consider, and pause, sometimes even for a moment, in wonder at what is. That means seeing the grain of wood or the stains on concrete as beautiful, but it also means seeing the sky that opens up where building stops and realizing the vast scale of what is not human. Good designers work in all sorts of ways to make us see what is there not only right in front of us, but out there.

Several decades after I had first encountered the Capp Street House (it has since been, ironically enough, restored and turned into a preserved version of its own preservation), I returned to the Bay Area for a party that two local collectors, Norah and Norman Stone, liked to give at their vineyard in Napa Valley every summer. They, too, had renovated an old house with art and skill, though here the preservation consisted more of carefully distressed lumber and raw walls coordinated and cleaned. They had also eschewed building a gallery space for their art, as some of their neighbors had, instead hollowing out a cave in a cliff next to their house and filling it with the latest works. The party started with a viewing of those pieces, with some of the artists in attendance to discuss their work (or the latest art-world gossip). Then we moved onto the lawn for dinner and, as the sun was setting, the best part of the evening started.

One of the artists in attendance was the Chicagoan Theaster Gates. Trained in urban planning at Kansas State, he had also studied theology and art, as well as apprenticing himself to a master ceramicist in Japan. He had returned to Chicago's South Side to work for the University of Chicago, which supported him in his art and community endeavors. These came together in a Midwest version of the Capp Street House, the Dorchester Project. Starting in 2009, Gates worked with local kids and artisans to collect materials he used to transform a small house into a community center. Both its inside and its exterior now consist of pieces of lumber and fragments of other buildings that bring some of their memories with them while creating a house that feels old, but uncertain in origin and purpose. Its core is a room where Gates stored a collection of back issues donated by *Ebony* magazine; it was a library not of the collected wisdom of Western philosophers and writers, but of the heritage central to the recent history of this African-American community.

The Dorchester Project, which Gates later riffed on in creating the Huguenot House for Documenta, the art expo in Kassel, Germany, was paid for by selling fragments that either were from its construction and deconstruction, or acted as analogies to what he was doing. It was also the venue for performances by the Delta Monks, a pick-up band of musicians, including Gates, who riffed on the varied traditions in which he grew up, from straight blues to jazz to rap.

As the light fell at the Stones' carefully composed house, the Delta Monks started playing on the porch, filling the night air with their own bricolage of sounds. They made an ephemeral architecture in which the textures of the music, its melodies, and its words evoked memories in the same manner as both Gates's or David Ireland's physical projects. It was a performance that was not just a musical event, but a collective experience, just as the architecture Gates had made consisted of art projects that used form, images, and spaces to evoke shared memories. You did not actually live the lives the artist evoked, but had access to them, in one particular time and place. That is a limitation, but it also made me think that bricolage can and must have exactly the same power as any great work of art in any medium if it is to have the ability to convince us of its worth. If architecture is to be not just the most efficient production of shelter, and not a monument to a dead person or a person's power, but something that draws us and our world together, helps us to understand where we have come from, where we are, and perhaps, where we are going, it must have the ability to amaze us into stunned contemplation, recognition, and wonder. Bricolage needs its own Pantheons and Rothkos.

As the sky went completely dark in Napa and the stars came out, the Delta Monks stopped playing and we drifted back onto the lawn for the last act of the evening. We went into locker rooms, took off our party clothes, and donned bathing suits. Then we dove into the swimming pool, as enticing as any suburban body of water on a hot summer evening, and paddled to its far end. A quick duck down, a few strokes, and you found yourself emerging into a tall room with water for a floor and sky for a ceiling. This was one of James Turrell's "Skyspaces," where all you do is sit (or, in this case, float), and watch what is usually all around you: sky. Turrell's trick consists in cutting the edge of the ceiling opening with such a thin frame that you see it as just a line, making the sky appear as a picture in a frame. Best seen at dawn or dusk, this slice of air not only changes color over time, but, as it does so, takes on a shape all its own, weighing down on you or opening up, depending on the color and amount of light. In recent years, Turrell has balanced and enhanced the effect with interior light, but I still prefer the pure rooms where the balance between the abstraction of the room and the fullness of nature works its magic.

In one night, we had gone from the polite contemplation of nice art and architecture, to being part of a momentary bricolage, to coming as close to having a sublime experience of space as might be possible in our modern world without leaving it all together. Driving back into town that evening, I asked myself: is there a relationship between these two seeming extremes, the architecture of the everyday and the time-bound, and the architecture of boundless nothingness revealed?

WHERE TO FIND CIVIC ARCHITECTURE

19 When architecture really works, it brings the everyday and the immeasurable together. We actually have a building type for that: the civic buildings at the core of our democracies. If our society is working well, we find ourselves gathering in and around structures that both house the operations of day-to-day government and make us see something bigger than what each of is individually: our collective landscape.

To find structures that work in that manner, you have to see them not only as objects, but as human answers to both the human-made and the natural landscape. I have driven all the way or part of the way across the United States half a dozen times, and have repeated this pattern of seeing while in motion across Europe, usually with some goal (moving to a new job or visiting a site), but also because I am always looking for these moments when awe comes out of the meeting of human endeavor with land, water, and sky.

The best way to experience the relationship between land, sky, nature, and human structures is by bicycle, because at that pace space unfolds around you in a way that you can comprehend as coherent but dynamic, while there are no barriers between you and what is around you. It also makes your muscles feel the actual contours of the land and regulates your speed according to the grid of human streets.

The car, however, offers a larger vista, where the repetition of reactions to the landscape in the rhythm of cross streets, towns, landmarks, and even billboards imprints itself into instant memories of a cultural skein thrown over the landscape. There is a combination of fundamental facts—such as the chasm that opens up when you cross a river, the slow approach to the Rocky Mountains that become, from a faint line on the horizon, a massive reality that fills your vision on all sides, or the sky that is everywhere always present in all its varieties—that is always with you. Then there are the human-made incidents, the remnants of old structures and the promise of new forms in the glass skyscrapers of city centers.

> You enforce that sense of both the sameness and the difference of things by stopping to eat food in chain stores and looking for local variations. As you slow down off the highway, familiar signs and forms—the McDonald's, the gas station, but also the grain silos of the Midwest or the barns of the East—mix with the particularities of the kinds of plants, flowers, and trees of that location, the stone cropping up underneath them, and the more ephemeral differences in light.

EVERY PLACE IS REAL, EVERY PLACE HAS A HISTORY, EVERY PLACE HAS A SENSE OF PLACE, EVEN AS EVERY PLACE IS ALSO MORE AND MORE THE SAME.

> Understanding this point through the repetition of the same drive or visit to a building reinforces a sense of how we as humans layer our civilization over and thread it through natural facets, creating a bricolage on not just a local, but a regional and even national, scale.

Every so often, you find a building that sums it up. For me, one of those was the Nebraska State Capitol, which I have visited several times. It sits in the middle of an urban grid like that of any other town in the United States. The city of Lincoln is flat, and not particularly distinguished—you can immediately understand the downtown, the government district, the university area, the residential areas layering from old and fancy, through the abandoned, to the new suburbs, with the fingers of railroad yards and industry cutting in near the core, and the schools and shopping malls spread out in dots sprinkling the outskirts—while natural topography modulates and differentiates the whole to be someplace that could only be Lincoln. It is a real place, with its own smell and taste, but one you can recognize.

In the middle, on the slightest of rises, sits the square block of the Capitol. It was designed by a New York architect, Bertram Goodhue, working with artists from elsewhere, in a style that you can best describe as stripped neo-classicism: big blocks with memories of classical orders. It was constructed out of local materials, however, and the decorations evoke bison and local trees. It is meant to be a celebration of what Nebraska and Lincoln are.

At its center is a tower almost 400 feet tall that proclaims the importance of Nebraska. You can see the tower from miles around, and it marks the spot where it all comes together. Elevators, decorated with motifs based on those developed by Native Americans who once lived here, take you up to the top, from which you can see all of the landscape coming together.

The tower has another function. Its tip is a dome, which makes it a vestigial marker of democracy, as domes signal such a legislative coming together in state capitols all across the United States. On top of the dome stands a statue of a sower, spreading his seed onto the fertile plain below. It is a phallic symbol of astonishing frankness, which elevates sexual power to the ability of humans to transform

what they perceive as female nature into masculine order. It shows
how primeval and how self-conscious we can become about making
a place our own. For a visitor such as me, it is one of those points
where my attempts to make sense of how we as humans use and see
our world suddenly becomes easy.

WHY YOU SHOULD DRIVE THE GRID

20 Why are people prepared to pay so much more for an item of
clothing or an accessory simply because of its label? For me, the
20th-century French artist Marcel Duchamp shed more light on this
question than any fashion commentator. It was 1917 when he infam-
ously scrawled the signature "R. Mutt" on the side of an upturned
urinal, titled it *Fountain*, and submitted it for exhibition as a work
of art. Duchamp believed that once it was labeled as art, the urinal
became art. *Fountain* was summarily rejected by the exhibition curators,
but Duchamp's theory that we value objects primarily because of
their label rather than their purpose became famous.

I had been trained to "read" the landscape by working on a historic
building survey in the Naugatuck Valley, a former industrial zone
in Connecticut where the rivers once powered mills that eventually
milled copper and gave rise to an ersatz leather called "naugahyde."
All summer long, I walked the towns of this valley, block by hot block,
noting down the distinguishing features of each building, classify-
ing it by style, and then, based on that information, guessing on the

date. I noted where the rich people's houses were, where the mill buildings had been placed, where the commercial streets ran, and how the orientation of urban grids and buildings changed over time. By the end of the summer, I could figure out the age of just about any building to within five years of its construction.

Having arrived in Cincinnati, I bought the cheapest car I could find and spent the weekend driving the grid. The city where I lived was a different place from most in the Midwest: founded as a fort and trading depot on the Ohio River, it sat in a bowl of what the natives like to think of as seven hills (as in Rome), but which are actually glacial moraines: the debris left over after the glaciers had scraped the terrain to the north into the flat landscape we now associate with the Midwest. That made this a place apart, a river town focused inward. I would leave this little bowl and rise in barely perceptible ramps on the highway up the terraces that these long-ago geological and climatological events had left behind, before turning off one of the big roads that course through the grid on a diagonal. I would head into one of the small towns and villages that dotted a landscape President Jefferson and his surveyors had imagined as the place for an American democracy.

The Jeffersonian grid, as we call it today, consists of "sections," each a mile square. A homestead within that grid was a quarter section. Jefferson's idea was that pioneers would be given such parcels to farm, thus spreading what he saw as an agrarian, cooperative civilization over an empty (apart from the untold tribes of Native Americans, who were soon pushed out of the way) terrain. He assumed that villages would form at certain intersections, and suggested that parcels be kept aside for such public functions as schools and court houses.

That actually happened, with the congregations occurring more often than not where the grid encountered a peculiarity of the natural terrain: a river or gorge that needed to be crossed, a hill rising above the landscape, or the presence of a natural resource such as water. A stretch of the grid would turn into a collection of commercial buildings that generally received the name Main Street, just as such strips were High Streets in England. A major intersection would become the site for a court house or county seat, often with a public square around it. The main churches would then arise around or near those two features. The wealthiest people would build their houses on the highest ground they could find. Mill buildings would develop near the water or on the approach into town.

Over the decades and even centuries, these original features have become embedded in towns that sprawl along the grid, and in many cases you can still find the germs of what was not a preset urban form, as in the American towns laid out according to the "Law of the Indies" under Spanish domination or the even older towns with Roman roots, but an ad hoc response to the intersection of an abstract order and a particular set of conditions. What is more, the buildings were created out of kits of parts. Starting in the middle of the 18th century, building techniques became standardized into what become known as the "balloon frame," which consisted of 2-inch by 4-inch wood "studs" in 8-foot lengths assembled in a lightweight and flexible frame that even semi-skilled craftspeople could build, with an overall form and façade often composed using pattern books brought from the East Coast. The commercial buildings were often made out of local bricks with standard ornamentation, and the industrial buildings out of whatever was cheapest and strongest at the time of construction.

As I drove from town to town, I kept recognizing almost the same street, almost the same corner, and almost the same house. Yet each was different, each represented its own intersection, each had changed through use over the years. No town was actually the same, no moment or space was exactly alike, but all were part of a pattern of settlement and were physical embodiments of the ways in which American daily life had evolved.

What had opened up this closed but flexible system was technology. The biggest buildings originally were the factories and mills that rose to transform the wealth of the land into finished products. Then came the railroads, slicing through the grid on their way to metropolises such as Cincinnati and, later, Chicago. Along their path rose the grain silos, towering over the towns, sited at the diagonal of the train, and proclaiming something other, something abstract, something stored and transformed. My favorite college teacher, the architectural historian Vincent Scully, had shown a comparison of Chartres Cathedral with a grain silo in one of his classes, and now I knew exactly what he meant: the wealth of the land transformed into and stored in a structure that rose up and against both the human and the natural landscape.

Later technologies have been less heroic, with the highways by passing the towns altogether, factories becoming anonymous sheds, and schools and businesses moving to the outskirts to take their place alongside strip malls that dissipate space and dissolve any sense of the grid's presence. Any trip into a small town in Ohio, Indiana, or Illinois was kind of archaeology, cutting through the layers of history that started with the retail strips, McDonald's, and cul-de-sac neighborhoods at the edge, to arrive at the core, now often empty and forlorn, a future ruin perhaps, giving testimony to a particular way in which humans made a place for themselves.

By reading this landscape, I came to see time and politics, lives lived and places made. The beauty I found was nostalgic and perhaps invented, but it made me love the simple act of building community.

WHERE TO FIND URBAN PATTERNS

21 One of the reasons you should drive, cycle, or walk the landscape is that its rhythms and patterns reveal themselves in a fundamental manner, and one layered in time and space. You truly know a place by moving through it and analyzing its various aspects at eye level. It is a different form of knowledge, but one that can become intertwined with the abstract analysis of reading and drawing. Knowing place in this manner lets you create a palimpsest of architecture, an interpretation and reimagining of place that I like to think of, however pretentiously and ephemerally, as its own architecture.

In 2001, I moved back to the Netherlands, where I had grown up between the ages of four and sixteen. It was a pleasure to rediscover that country and to be able to hop on a train and be in Paris in four hours, or to visit London by plane for lunch and be home in time for dinner. But what really excited me was the discovery of a whole new terrain that previously had been off-limits to me: Eastern Europe. When I was growing up, it was behind an Iron Curtain and, like the fascist dictatorships of Greece and Spain, out of bounds.

When I started going there, I also discovered—or perhaps imagined—patterns. I first noticed them in Prague, but I saw the same from Ljubljana in Slovenia to some of the older towns in Poland. Even the old Austrian town of Salzburg, for instance, had the same order. What I noticed was that these cities were founded on a bend in the river below a high rock or cliff. That is where the castle—which, in the case of Prague, turned into a palace and later the home of the president, and in Budapest into a cultural complex—is situated. The old town below is a warren of streets that have grown up by tying the landing spots in the river to the access points to the rock, as well as to everything from the first well to the cathedral or church, to the roads around the rock and the agricultural fields beyond. They reflect the complex relations between humans and the natural settings.

Across the river, things are different. Usually laid out under Hapsburg, Prussian, or Russian rule, these settlements (the New Town in both Prague and Budapest) spread out in a grid, reflecting the fact that an outside ruler planned them in one go. A bridge, such as the Charles Bridge in Prague, leads to a small square on an embankment, and from there axes connect one public space to another (Prague, in this case, is slightly different because there already was an established settlement on that spot, causing the grid to be incomplete and skewed). Around the major squares you will find those buildings that both symbolize and further the imperial culture into which these cities were assimilated: the opera, the theater, the concert hall, the university, the museum, and the parliament or palace of the governor. Each one of these was designed according to the dictates of a universal language of building, in this case usually a baroque version of neo-classicism, complete with columns, pediments, grand stairs, central and side pavilions, and ornament that proclaims the importance of everything from great statesmen to local composers. The meat of the new city matter, meanwhile, consists of fairly uniform blocks of apartments, their ground floors taken up by retail and restaurants, and many of them since converted into or replaced by office buildings.

At the edge of this 17th- to 19th-century city is usually a park, which is often the site of more cultural monuments or diversions such as a zoo. It formed a buffer to the poorer neighborhoods that sprung up on the outskirts, and offered the city dwellers a domesticated version of nature. Everything, including that nature, was under control, everything was of a piece, everything created an atmosphere, as well as a rhythm to life, that conformed to standards developed at a court someplace far away.

Then the avenue that led out of the New Town through the park became broader and was extended farther out, sometimes after World War I, but more often during the period of Soviet occupation. At the other end of the park new stadia and cultural centers of a vast scale arose. Their forms were abstract, though sometimes sculptures of heroic workers reminded visitors of the ideals to which they had to aspire. They sought to defy gravity and the norms established by the imperialists. Instead, they offered machines that would transform citizens into members of the proletariat that would build a new society.

From there, block after block of housing marched on into the countryside. Often built using a system developed in East Germany (*plattenbau*, which means "panel building"), they are identical concrete slabs inside of which every dwelling is the same. They stand at angles, defying both the grid and the natural topography. This was a new world, about as far away in both distance and attitude as you could get from the Old Town huddling between the castle and the river. In recent years, a new chapter has been added to this process, spreading, abstracting, and growing from the original kernel. Some of the Soviet blocks have been torn down to make way for shopping malls or luxury housing, and beyond the range of blocks sprawl appears, little different from what you find in the rest of Europe or, for that matter, the world. Here, order and scale get jumbled, clarity disappears, and only the signs that tell you what to buy or where to go give any direction. This is the realm you move through by car and in which you are always plugged into global systems. Whatever was the original place that gave rise to this whole urban system matters little. It remains only as a memory of itself and as a tourist destination.

Looking at a town, whether a small one in America's Midwest or a large one in Eastern Europe, can give you a history lesson. It can help you understand what the landscape was, and how people reacted to its features. It lets you see where power and money were, how order and a common culture arose or were imposed, and how that specific set of developments—always fed, we should not forget, by global networks of communications and trade—has now dissolved into sameness everywhere, always dissolving into forms that are increasingly difficult to understand.

I have long believed that architecture is not just a tool to understand and make buildings. It is a way to see and know your world through the physical manifestations of what our predecessors have made out of it. Buildings, especially in relation to each other and the natural landscape, both on the inside and the outside, are artifacts that, if we look at them hard enough, allow us to understand our culture in the same deep way that literature, philosophy, painting, or history can.

ONCE WE TRULY KNOW WHAT WE HAVE MADE, WE THEN HAVE THE POWER TO DO WHAT IS TRULY NECESSARY, NAMELY TO CHANGE THE WORLD WE HAVE INHERITED.

WHY UNDERSTANDING SPRAWL MATTERS

22 Where we should start changing the world is with the landscape that it is most difficult to understand. Since World War II, a tide of ticky-tacky houses has spread out from almost every major metropolis in the world. These constructions have very little relation to their particular sites. Although they might look slightly different in the United States than they do in Europe or Asia, the principles are the same. Developers buy up land, flatten it, remove whatever is there, and put up houses that are all more or less the same and often identical. Built as cheaply as possible, they have become bigger, but not better, over the years. They can usually work only because of air conditioning and other technology. Finally, they are laid out not according to a grid that would draw them into a larger whole, nor in relation to the land, but to create inward-turned groupings that make people feel both safe and free.

Around these developments similar clumps grow up: clusters of office buildings and warehouses, shopping malls set in acres of parking, and strip malls that have dissolved the streets along which they run. Even civic monuments look like anonymous commercial structures, and schools are bunkers that often have no windows. These days, at least in the United States, it is usually only hospitals that have some verve or twist that distinguishes them on the outside, even if their innards are also all the same. I assume that is because they have more money.

> When you go out into these suburbs and exurbs, it is easy to get lost. You are where you are nowhere. Even the materials and colors are the same—in the United Kingdom a kind of cheap brick, in the United States a stucco substitute called Dryvit. If you were to do a color sample of a standard American suburb, you would get a gradation that runs between brown and gray. Only the signs stand out, proclaiming the primacy of commerce.

There is a serious problem underlying this ugliness. Such developments are hugely destructive of the land and waste natural resources at a vast scale—not just in their construction, but also because we have to commute around them all day in cars. What is more, they separate us from each other as we sit in our little cocoons at work or home, plugged into electricity and the internet, connecting only on errands or regularized play dates and exercise routines.

> This sprawl is not going to go away. We have to understand it and figure out how to make it better. I do not know anybody who has figured out how to do it. I taught a design studio at the University of Michigan a number of years ago in which I asked the graduate students to design a square mile of sprawl on Detroit's far exurbs. The studio was one of the worst failures of my career.

I am fascinated by sprawl: I hate it, and I want to understand it and know what to do about it. That should be one of the central tasks of architecture.

WHERE IT ALL COMES TOGETHER

23 In sprawl, you can find the building blocks that might help make the environment better. To find them you have to travel far and aimlessly since our human habitations now cover the countryside. Luckily, I love exploring sprawl.

For some people, a vacation means going to a beach or a lake and doing ... well, I am not exactly sure. I have tried that a few times, and amused myself by reading or writing, but my idea of a truly great time is to get on the road, by plane, car, train, or bus, and to read the landscape. Like any tourist, I find the landmarks, but it is what you find along the way that is just as important. The United States, a nation that is always on the move, has left markers of that restlessness along the road not only in literature and film, but also in the countless motels, restaurants, and the other paraphernalia of travel. In Europe, the layering of historical landscapes is often so intense that you can see the traces of four or five cultures at one roadside stop. In Asia, you can track the remains of old pilgrimage routes and imperial roads.

I go to visit what others might think are odd markers. In the American Midwest, I noticed that in many places the high school was often the first piece of modernism to make its way into town. Often built on the outskirts, on a hill, it consists of one- to two-story brick buildings with windows set in metal sashes. They have little ornament, and their proportions emphasize the horizontal and open the classes up to light and air without overwhelming the students in the way the older buildings often did. The wings are offset, sometimes in pinwheels, to create interior courtyards that are still open to the outside. Canopies connect the parts and are supported on metal poles. An administration block sits behind the main entrance, but the big shape is the gymnasium, which doubles as an auditorium. It turns out that one firm (Perkins & Wills of Chicago) was responsible for a remarkable number of these schools, but the type spread all over the country. It became what several generations who grew up learning in them associated with the new world, one that they otherwise might only see in the big city. These structures have an optimism that comes out of their very simplicity and the play of their abstract forms.

Contrast that with the ornate structures of the fifty U.S. state capitols. (I have seen a little over half of them, including the one in Lincoln, Nebraska, which is a bit of an exception.) Almost every other one has the same elements: a central cupola or dome, which denotes democracy; side wings to house the various chambers of the state legislature and sometimes the court; layers of cells for bureaucrats around those ceremonial spaces on every side (including below and above) to turn them into blocks; and grand stairs leading up the structure, which usually sits on a hill. I love traveling from, say, Colorado's rather bland and staid version of this type of building to the ornate Wisconsin State Capitol, which sits in the middle of Madison, forcing the traffic around it and dissolving inside into a collection of stones from every state, and passage ways and balconies where you can sense the deals being done.

At a smaller scale, I love going to see how, in the Midwest, modernist banks came to replace their neo-classical predecessors, moving to street corners to accommodate the car, and breaking the block with angles and glass windows. In Eastern Europe, almost every town had at least one modernist architect who had studied in Berlin, Vienna, or Paris and who came back to compose white walls and corner windows into villas for the progressive rich during the period between the two world wars. In China, I had my students catalog the variations on the basic housing block and found out that there were only six, from which just about every apartment building complex from Hong Kong to Beijing is constructed.

Finding these patterns, forms, and rhythms that shape our daily lives lets you understand how economic and state forces work; how commerce and power spread and install themselves in communities, becoming a reality that is lived every day.

ARCHITECTURE STOPS BECOMING ABOUT MONUMENTS AND TURNS INTO THE NODES THAT FOCUS OUR LIVES, METING OUT SPACE, POWER, AND ROLES FOR EVERYBODY.

WHAT WE CAN STILL LEARN FROM THE GREEKS

24 Both the power of positioning individual buildings in the landscape and the attraction of the nodal development of a place in relation to that landscape have ancient roots. Last summer, I returned to the place where much of this started, at least for those of who live in or are shaped by the culture of Western Europe. I had been to Greece as a high-school student, backpacking my way from one classical monument to another. I had understood little of what I visited, because I had not learned to see buildings (or, in this case, the remains of buildings) in relation to their site. Now I returned to Athens, Delphi, Olympia, Epidaurus, Mycenae, Corinth, and a few places in between, to see if I could perceive how it all started.

I carried with me an electronic copy of Vincent Scully's first book, *The Earth, the Temple, and the Gods*. I had read it as an undergraduate and I perused fragments of it again now, trying to understand the places and what the ancient Greeks had made out these sites.

Scully points out that the culture we think of as classical Greece had developed in the main part of the country, from the Peloponnese to the north of Athens, in no more than half a dozen valleys. These spaces were all remarkably similar in size and nature. They were large enough to contain sizable communities supported by agriculture, but were always in sight of both the sea and the surrounding mountains. Those mountains spurred out into ridges or gave rise to isolated outposts such as the one on which the Acropolis in Athens stands, and it was these sites that became the places where the religious and political structures that we still admire today arose. What is most remarkable is the way in which these buildings stand in relation to their settings. They command the part of the valley they are in, but they also respond to the mountains behind or around them. Scully developed a theory (and I here bowdlerize his much more complex points) about how many of the early temples and ritual sites lined up with the space between two hills or mountains, which represented either the breasts of the earth deity or the horns of the sky god. After that first alignment, subsidiary temples then developed not in direct alignment with the first built fact, but at angles, so as to create an active space that brought the rhythm of the surrounding landscape down into the field on which the temples stood, while letting them dispose themselves as objects that you experience as such, rather than merely as façades seen from the front or the side.

I saw this logic at work in site after site. I also saw the ways in which structures were tied to a specific natural setting and its features, which they repressed or replaced: the cave underneath Delphi's Temple of Apollo, where (as current theories will have it) gasses from the mountains leaked out to intoxicate the soothsayers making their Delphic pronouncements; or a similar site in Epidaurus, where sick people would be put to sleep in a dark undercroft to awaken healed by that deep rest. The slopes at both those sites had become transformed and regularized into arenas and theaters where games and plays could be staged, turning the abstract play of nature or the gods into their human equivalent, where what was out of our control could be played out.

There are only ruins left of these buildings, but those few fragments let us understand this kind of basic and fundamental architecture. There are equivalents in every culture but, in Europe, everything started here.

WHY WE SHOULD BUILD WITH (AND NOT ON) THE LAND

25 A trip back to basics can make us wonder about architecture before buildings that stand on their own. Architecture is not just a way to create an individual shelter: it is a way to mark, know, and establish a deep belonging in the landscape. We have to figure out how that was done and how we could do that again.

The Europeans created places such as Stonehenge; and in America the Anasazi built dwellings including Mesa Verde, Canyon de Chelly, and Chaco Canyon, while the Hopi built Taos Pueblo, and the Fort Ancient culture constructed the Great Serpent Mound of Ohio. Each of them ties the landscape and culture together in a manner that belies the ways in which later settlers have laid their grids, roads, and isolated houses on them.

The Great Serpent Mound is the only one of these sites that is purely ceremonial. Its setting is remarkable. Standing on its highest point, you can see a uniform line of hills in the distance all around you; the area was the site of meteorite impact at one point, and it left an immense bowl in the middle of which the Mound sits. You feel as if you are in the middle of the world because the setting and the architecture serve to center you and, looking around, I kept confusing my cultures. This resembles Eden, and the serpent must be the one that gave Eve the apple, causing us to roam forever? I know that is not correct, but this sense of a primeval connection to the land in a form that rises out of and is barely distinguishable from the geology it marks evokes such associations.

The other sites created by those who populated the North American continent long before European settlers arrived are towns that have a very particular relationship to the land. All except for Taos are part of that land, tracing its contours. Mesa Verde is built into the cliffs around it, while Chaco Canyon houses rows of semicircular dwellings that follow the curves of the canyon walls behind them. This is architecture that builds with, rather than on, the land, elaborating the natural setting into the orders and rhythms of human settlement.

Taos Pueblo consists of two artificial mounds, or villages, around a stream. Scully, who continued his work on Greek temples by looking at these sites, argued that these two settlements mimicked two of the peaks of the Sangre de Cristo Mountains, from which the small stream ultimately emanates.

Each of these villages is also—like the earliest multi-family dwellings we know in Turkey, the Indus Valley, and China—a collective structure. Houses are built on top of each other, and you move not through separate streets but on shared patios and roofs. It makes you aware of an important fact about architecture: when it stops consisting of tents that you carry with you, it turns into a shared structure with a direct relationship to the site in which you settle. I think we should always remember that the roots of human habitation are in and act as responses to the landscape; either it is a hunting and gathering of nature together, weaving it into the temporary settlements that move with you or dissolve back into the ground, or it is a tracing, tracking, marking, and measuring of the landscape in a manner that connects you directly to that place, but only fully as a member of a collective culture.

That model is so important exactly because Western settlers ignored it so thoroughly. The archetypal American home—as another acute critic of the landscape, J. B. Jackson, pointed out—stands against the landscape, raising itself as a self-enclosed, vertical structure that has a direct relationship to the orders humans have made. In the Midwest, the Jeffersonian grid gives rise to the isolated farmhouse in each plot, oriented toward the road that follows that grid according to an order that rarely goes out of its way for any natural contour. Later, that grid became one of power and water lines, connecting each isolated structure through technology to a whole that might exist far over the horizon.

The house itself consists, as I noted, of bits and pieces that are generic and standardized. The most solid element would be the chimney: the vertical element that gathered the family together in this isolated shelter and proclaimed the presence of that fragment of a community to the outside world.

Such houses were cheap, easy to change, and easy to abandon, as happened all too often when settlers moved further west. Americans might not build in this manner much any more (although two-by-fours are still the standard for most suburban construction), but they gave rise to the model of American inhabitation of the land in isolated structures, light and cheap, that turn inward and away from both each other and the landscape around them. There is a beauty to such structures, but the aim of architecture has always been to open them back up to each other and to the landscape. The "shingle style," which elaborated on the "stick style" of early balloon-frame homes, emphasized the spread of rooms, open to each other and the landscape, underneath roofs that traced and tracked the land below. Frank Lloyd Wright elaborated that style in his Prairie School homes, and ever since then COUNTLESS ARCHITECTS HAVE TRIED TO FIND WAYS TO ATONE FOR THE ORIGINAL SIN OF AMERICAN ARCHITECTURE, which ate the apple of independence and economy, and slithered away from its Edenic setting into the isolating and alienating grids that promised the artificial connection of democracy.

HOW TO BUILD LANDSCRAPERS

26 Most buildings just sit on the land. Building with the land would be much better. If you think of buildings as being an extension and intensification of the landscape, you will site them in such a way that they do less harm to the existing environment. You will also be able to handle rain, snow, and heat more easily. Finally, building with the land means that the finished structure will not be alien.

Some of the best buildings I have ever visited are, like the Alhambra, essentially landscapes with a framework that you can also inhabit. But not many buildings have large enough sites or thin enough programs to be able to be just courtyards and gardens. So we wind up plunking down our structures on the land. Sometimes we cut a courtyard through them, and perhaps we open up views to the surrounding environment, but in constructing them we are always removing part of what was once a shared site and reserving it for the use of those who are allowed to enter. Then we also have to get rid of the water that used to run through or under the site, the snow that lay there as a blanket, or the weeds that grew there. This makes for more walls and lines of separation as we dig drainage ditches and other defensive mechanisms.

Some architects try to get rid of those distinctions. They bury as much of their buildings as possible underground, which also helps to insulate them. They plant the roofs with gardens. They find ways to enhance the existing site and even strengthen it—with a retaining wall or catch basin for water, a shaded copse or allée, or a place to shelter from the wind. They even make buildings that extend the landscape, offering a human-made version of what is there.

The architect Antoine Predock came up with a name for such buildings: landscrapers. He used it to describe a cultural center he designed in his native New Mexico. Rising out of the ground as a thin wedge, it offered a human-made answer to the mesas and ridges in which it appeared. Predock went on to design many structures that exhibited the same ability to unfold out of the land into an abstract version of the fields, hills, and other geologic features around them.

One of my favorite landscrapers is the Diamond Ranch School in Pomona, California, designed by Thom Mayne of Morphosis architects and finished in 2000. The massive high school is a series of folded ridges making up the roofs under which the classrooms and other functions shelter. Mayne obtained the geometry for the design by analyzing the contour lines of the hill on which the school sits. He turned those sinewy lines into straight cuts, then lifted and dropped them in turn to fit the rooms underneath. The shapes also evoke the endless staccato rhythm of the suburban homes that surround the school, here blown up to a monumental scale. Both the human-made and the natural landscape become visible in a clear manner. You can see and you can inhabit where you are. To make that all the more possible, Mayne cut canyons between the classroom buildings, opening them into plazas where you are surrounded by this new version of the landscape. You are in and of the place, but that place has also unfolded into something newer and larger.

Recently I was on the jury for a new resort that will be built on an artificial island off the coast of Hainan, China. The site is absurd: an expanse of sand the developer created in the middle of the sea, connected to the mainland and other islands only by thin bridges. Most architects who entered the competition, including Mayne, designed various towers and blocks that could have been placed anywhere exactly because the site had no particular characteristics that could inform their design.

The scheme offered by New York architects Diller Scofidio + Renfro was different. They noticed the curving shape of the island and the fact that, with a harbor dug in one side, it resembled a ying/yang symbol. They chose to enhance that geometry and to mark it by grouping almost all the several million square feet of program together into a single, curved structure that started out very low and rose to the equivalent of twenty stories. As they marked the island's main characteristic and made it visible and inhabitable in three dimensions, they also made the site's edges fuzzy, reserving them for marshes and mangrove swamps.

The architects' design for the Ecoisland (as the client called the project) was a breath of fresh air: a way of building on new land at a massive scale, as happens all too often in Asia, but in a manner that would let us enjoy both the artifice and the potential of such places. The project may never be built (the client thought it was awfully strange), but I hope it will inspire more landscrapers.

HOW TO BUILD A COMMUNITY

27 In 1932, Frank Lloyd Wright decided to build his own version of an American Eden. It would be dedicated to architecture—or rather, to remaking America through architecture. "Truth Against the World" was the Wright family's motto, and he felt that his building designs embodied that verity. He didn't just design buildings: he broke boxes, or so he said, and made shrines to the American family that would let it become the building block for a reborn version of Jefferson's democratic landscape, which Wright called "Usonia."

To start things off, he founded what has been the most successful and enduring architecture workshop in the world: Taliesin. (I am currently the president of its present-day iteration, the Frank Lloyd Wright School of Architecture at Taliesin.)

What Wright had in mind was a community of makers. He invited young men and women to join him at his family farm in Spring Green, Wisconsin, which he had already transformed into a combination of home, farm, and atelier. He added a school building he had designed for his aunts several decades earlier to his resources, turning that into a drafting room and dormitory for the apprentices, who paid him for the pleasure of working his farm, keeping his household, building additions, and helping him to draft up and supervise the construction of the buildings he designed.

It was a commune where everybody worked, ate, and (often in both senses of the word) slept together. They also performed music, dance, and theater, as Wright felt that architecture was part of a wider culture. Although the Fellowship, as it came to be known, tended toward a cult—and certainly became one during the more than two decades his widow, Olgivanna, ran it after he passed away in 1959—it also produced extraordinary architecture.

Taliesin itself was and is a signal example of how architecture can embody the ideal of a community. Its various buildings nestle into the hillsides of an area called the Driftless Region, which the glaciers passed by during the last ice age. The main house is a ramble of rooms that spreads across the brow of the hill ("Taliesin" means "shining brow" in Welsh), lording it over the valley where Wright grew up. Inside, the spaces flow around piers that both anchor the floating domestic scene and focus it around stone fireplaces. The home is a collective place to gather, view, order, and be ordered by the building's framework.

> The Hillside School is simpler affair, its square space of gathering rising to a pyramid-shaped roof. The drafting room sits next door, its wood and steel trusses offering a lesson in connections and spans while letting light in, and its bunk rooms shelter this place of creativity with their rows of wood-lined monks' cells. Taliesin is the American home turned into a civic complex and put back into relationship with the landscape.

In 1937, Wright built a winter home for the Fellowship. Called Taliesin West and located on another brow, a mesa overlooking Phoenix below the McDowell Mountains, it is a more integrated complex. It is also a more ephemeral one. Originally, the buildings were tents: canvas stretched between redwood frames set at an angle on concrete bases Wright shaped out of the desert and its rocks. You originally approached them in a spiral, moving around and up the desert landscape, seeing glimpses of the angles and the low base walls of "desert concrete" against the jagged line of the mountains, until you arrived at a rock inscribed with Native American petroglyphs. Fellows had found the rock on the site and Wright had it moved to this position, marking a continuity with the Native Americans' signing of their interpretation of the land they occupied.

> From that point, you moved up a few steps and past buildings set at an angle to each other in a horizontal and more regular version of the Greek temple sites. Taliesin West's main axis lines up with distant cinder cones and traces the main ridge of the mountains behind it, while other structures angle away to occupy the site's spread. Here the office, drafting room, Wright's house, and the structures the main

Fellows occupied become condensed into a single structure that rambled like the Spring Green complex, but also cohered like the collective structures the Anasazi had built.

Taliesin West's insides are ephemeral spaces (or were; the canvas has been replaced by glass and plastic, the wood by steel) that are still rooted to the site, both in their base and in their orientation. They look out toward distant views and into sheltered patios.

The students, meanwhile, live in what were originally Basque shepherders' tents. Over the years they have turned into more elaborate structures, which the new apprentices build themselves. The ones that work or are considered beautiful by subsequent students are reused and adapted; the others fall apart, back into the desert. They are each an experiment in how you make yourself at home in the desert and in what is by now part of Phoenix's suburban sprawl. When I arrived at Taliesin, I made that construction mandatory again after a lapse of several years, and asked each student to develop a thesis around the structure's design, construction, and occupation that would speculate on what that means. How can we be at home in a landscape we have so long ignored, that we do not have the faculties to truly understand, and that we understand and use only through the application of massive amounts of technology?

I hope that we can thus continue what I think is one of the most heroic attempts in modern architecture to come to terms with these questions. Is it possible to use the particular knowledge and history of buildings in relationship to the landscape so that we can experience an order that shelters space we occupy collectively, while framing a relationship to both the human-made and the natural landscape? Can we find a way to be at home in sprawl?

HOW TO BREAK THE BOX

28 What Frank Lloyd Wright did, above all else, was to, as he put it, break the box. He did so in his designs for normal suburban homes, as well as civic monuments such as churches, and literally opened them up. We all live and work, and often play, in boxes. Walls enclose us, roofs shelter us, and floors support us. We enter through doors and look out through windows. These structures make us feel at home, but they also isolate us from each other and our world.

Frank Lloyd Wright did something very simple. He strengthened the notion of shelter and blew up the notion that it had to be a box. His roofs spread out, taking us under their wings. Fireplaces and nooks focused almost every room he designed around a core of coziness. Rooms where you perform basic functions, such as sleeping or going to the bathroom, are minimal. Places where you gather are larger and open up under those roofs toward windows that he placed in rows and—most radically of all—in corners, like in the Schroeder House. They draw your eye out into the landscape, connecting to everything that is there, from the trees and the sky to the neighbors walking down the street. His best houses, like the Robie House (finished in 1909) or Fallingwater (1937), make you feel completely at home and dangerously exhilarated as you find yourself drawn out beyond the safety of their structures.

The architect Le Corbusier, who was in many ways the opposite of Frank Lloyd Wright, had a formula for reproducing this effect. In his "Five Points for Architecture," first published in the 1920s, he suggested that, first, a house should be lifted off the ground. This would leave the ground open for services and storage, would get you off the cold or up to where you could find breezes. Thus you had your own new place. Once there, you should be able to see your surroundings through continuous strips of windows. The whole horizon would be yours. The house should also have a free plan, so that the activities of everyday life could flow in a natural way. Columns would organize the structure, leaving the space free around their rational grid. Finally, your roof should not just shelter you, but be a roof garden. It would be a human-made version of nature, lifted off the ground and modern.

THESE TWO VISIONS, ONE EMPHASIZING SHELTER AND ONE FREEDOM, SHARE A BELIEF IN ARCHITECTURE AS SOMETHING THAT SHOULD MAKE YOU FEEL AT HOME AT THE SAME TIME AS FREEING YOU.

It should not be about constructing containers and containment, but about giving you the confidence to be liberated.

HOW TO MAKE ARCHITECTURE THAT IS OF THE PLACE

29 If you are going to make an architecture that pervades and shapes every part of the environment, then make it into a special place that justifies the design not from the vision of the architect who wants to subject the inhabitant's every waking moment to some grand plan, but from a vision of how design can connect you to the place, its surroundings, and other inhabitants.

One of my favorite examples of such a place is Timberline, a ski lodge built between 1936 and 1938 on the timberline of Mount Hood, about an hour outside of Portland, Oregon. The building is grand and the setting magnificent, but what really makes being there into an amazing experience is the manner in which every aspect of the place tells you how it was made, and sometimes by whom, and then acts as a way to bring the larger world of the forests and mountains around you inside.

Timberline is the sort of building that I love because, first, it responds to its setting by offering a human-made version of the mountain behind it. Spreading out from a peaked turret into long ridges that embrace you as you come in, it rises out of a base made out the stones the workmen found on the site to a line of lighter-colored wood panels before a shingle roof contains the whole. It is both an artificial ridge and a giant version of a home, here turned into an expression of the collective enjoyment of nature.

The real revelation is the inside. The National Parks Service built Timberline as a make-work project during the Great Depression, and it not only hired hundreds of workers to lay the roads, create the ski lifts, and build the lodge, but also employed scores of artists and artisans to turn the whole site into a human-made version of the surroundings. The public rooms, mostly two-, three-, and four-story halls lined with wood and focused on wood chimneys, are filled with furniture that not only recalls the long tradition of "rustic" designs that replicated the chairs and tables trappers built themselves out of the wood and bark they found, but is also carved and decorated with plant and animal motifs taken from the woods outside. Beavers gnaw away at newel posts and fir trees become metal grates.

> The motifs continue in every room, where the team of artists crafted each bed, bedspread, lamp, and desk. Native American motifs mix with patterns the artists derived from rugs they found in the area, and each room has a watercolor drawing of one of the plants you can find outside. In the public rooms, you are part of a human-made forest, while in your room you are in doll's house version of the larger world. You feel as if you are living in an abstraction of your surroundings, turned into a shelter that cocoons you with wood and worked textures that, because of their designs, also connect you directly to the nature around you.

Timberline shows that great architecture can make you feel comfortable without being disconnected. It makes you part of a larger social whole, like the collective dwellings of earlier cultures, that echoes the natural world. It lets you understand where you are, not just in an intellectual way, but also by seeing, touching, and even hearing and smelling the woods and the rocks. The experience is a fleeting one, as befits our society. You stay at Timberline only for a few nights at most, and perhaps even just for an hour after coming down the mountain on your skis, but you still have that moment of deep connection through the framework of architecture.

HOW ARCHITECTURE
CAN BE TASTED

30 Years ago, Antoine Predock used to show himself skiing off the roofs of houses he was designing. He also would speak of his love of road cuts, telling us that he would stop and look at every layer, up to the crushed beer cans and cigarette butts at the top that denoted human settlement. Once, when Los Angeles was shut down because of civil unrest, he strapped on his skates and rollerbladed to the office. He said later that not only did it let him make it to a client meeting in another city, but it made him understand that the airport was not some abstract place, but part of the same landscape where his office was located.

I was reminded of how deep the knowledge of a place can be when I visited the Dominus Winery in Napa Valley not too long after it was finished. The structure could not be simpler, or so it would seem. It is a long box with a hole cut out roughly (but not quite) in the middle. It is not a solid form: the architects, the Swiss firm of Herzog & de Meuron, gathered rocks they found in a quarry a few miles away and then piled them into walls held together by gabions, which are the three-dimensional nets they use in the Alps to keep stones from falling on the roads they cut through the mountains. The Winery stands against the Mayacamas Mountains (which, in reality, are low hills), emphasizing and regularizing the ridge while marking the plateau of the Rutherford Bench, the best winemaking area in the Napa Valley. Because it is open, the structure merges the rough clods and vineyards of the Bench with the vertical forms of the hills behind. Deep inside this open box there are closed, air-conditioned spaces, creating a functional area where modern equipment works its magic on those grapes. Thus a double layer of glass and stones surrounds you when you are inside, making it clear that the Winery is of its place, but that it is using a technology of great complexity to turn the specifics of the place into something completely different: a complex and deep wine.

That day, after I had toured the building, its owner and winemaker, Christian Moueix, took me out to tour the vineyards themselves. We were walking around admiring the vines, which looked almost ready for the harvest, when his foreman came up to him. They started arguing about something, and pretty soon were picking up bits of soil, crumbling it in their hands, and then finally putting pieces in their mouths. Moueix ended the argument with a Gallic shrug, turned to me, and offered me a clod: "He says it taste too musty, but I think it is too acidy. What do you think?"

The expertise to be able to make any sort of judgment was far beyond me, but I tasted the earth. And, in so doing, it made me aware in a whole new way of the forms I was seeing. Then, when we tasted the wine that was made in the Herzog & de Meuron building using grapes grown in that soil, I tasted a different version of that same landscape.

HOW TO COOK UP BUILDINGS

31

Architecture is like cooking. I like that analogy a lot more than I do the comparison architects make all too often, which is to music.

ARCHITECTURE IS NOT JUST AN ABSTRACTION FLOATING
IN THE AIR. IT IS A PHYSICAL, ROOTED THING THAT SMELLS
AND SOUNDS AS MUCH AS IT LOOKS.

I have noticed that a remarkable number of architects love to cook as well as to eat. There is something about the way in which cooking takes materials from nature, collects and orders them, and then transforms them through the application of technology into something that reflects its origins but is very much human-made that is much like architecture. Or perhaps it is just that architects are sensualists who like to sublimate their appetites through the ritual of cooking, which calms, orders, and justifies this pure enjoyment of the physical while celebrating our ability to transform that earth.

When I am teaching, I therefore often find myself using cooking metaphors. Figuring out how finely to chop a program to bring out its texture; boiling the components down until they are unified but not mushy; figuring out how to give something a covering that seals in the juices but satisfies you when you bite into it; how to make something crunchy—all these are ways I try to guide students when they are designing a building.

It is not just about making the food. One of the first field trips I took to find satisfying pieces of architecture was with the architect Charles Moore. We careened around the countryside of Connecticut, Massachusetts, and New Hampshire in a caravan of cars, looking for colonial churches and Moore's own houses. Moore was in the lead, and so now and then he would veer off the road, forcing us all to follow him. He would park, sniff the air around a nondescript clam shack, and walk in. They would turn out to have the best fried clams in the area. Over the years, I have found that most architects have similar obsessions with food. The film director Peter Greenaway, himself obsessed with architecture, even made a movie in 1987 called *The Belly of the Architect*, whose set piece is what looks like a scrumptious dinner the eponymous hero stages in front of one of history's greatest lessons in form and space, the Pantheon in Rome. Cooking and eating complement architecture. They offer a scale of control and directness buildings can't offer. They appeal to senses that architects can't touch. (Ever licked a building? Don't try.) The best, of course, is when the two come together, and it is no coincidence that some of the best spaces architects have produced have been restaurants. Stages for social gathering, they are frameworks in which all the senses come together. The Four Seasons restaurant in New York, which closed in 2016, offered refined, modernist versions of classic food—each component working to reveal its inner nature and developing into complex combinations—in a room that teased sensuality out of glass, steel, leather, wood, and a bit of crystal. If I had to name one place where I felt truly modern, that would be it.

HOW SPATIAL ARRANGEMENT WORKS

32 Many architects are sensitive to the power of nature and its visceral pleasures; for me, this may be because I grew up in an artificial landscape. When I was four and we moved from Montana, a state of mountains, forests, lakes, and prairies, to the Netherlands, I was transported to what had once been a primeval swamp and is now one of the most densely populated and ordered places in the world. There I yearned for nature, for woods bigger than the little parks around our house and for views that came from heights. When we drove south for vacations, my face would be glued to the car window, waiting for the first sign of any kind of hill.

It was only much later, when I had moved away from home to go to college, that I came to realize the peculiar beauty of the Dutch landscape. I had appreciated the fullness of the meadows, sliced into rectangles by irrigation ditches and populated by cows in beautifully contrasting black and white, but it was when I experienced American sprawl in its fullest that I came to understand the beauty of the totally human-made environment.

There is an old saying that God made the world, but the Dutch made the Netherlands. That is, in many ways, quite true. The first historical mentions of what is now the Netherlands describe a delta region, not unlike the marshes of the Nile or the bayous of Louisiana. It was a place where land, water, and air mixed in a misty marsh of which only one small part, an area called the Biesbosch, still survives. In the early Middle Ages, farmers began reclaiming the land. They did so through a particular technique called "poldering," in which they built dikes out into the water, surrounded a bit of lake, sea, or marsh, and then pumped the water out of the pond they had made. The soil they eventually uncovered was rich in nutrients, giving them productive agricultural land.

Building and maintaining these polders took collective effort. The pumps had to run continuously to keep the water from seeping back in, and the dikes had to be maintained to withstand erosion and storms. This, in turn, created a political system based on such collaboration and on the use of technology rather than on a hierarchy focused on accumulating wealth in one place and on war. It also made for a very individual landscape that consisted of grids of meadows, each particular to the body of water they had replaced, surrounded by levees or dikes. Within these human-made ridges, the land was cut through with irrigation ditches that were used for drainage, and pervaded by a technology of sluices, weirs, and, at first, windmills to keep the pumps going.

> Two-thirds of the Netherlands' main area, the provinces of North and South Holland and Utrecht, is below sea level and would sink back into marsh if this system was not maintained. That landscape is thus completely created by humans. Wherever you look, in the vistas made famous by 17th-century Dutch painters, you might see grass and a few trees, but what you are actually observing is a giant artifice.

As humans made this landscape, humans can also remake it. There is no primeval forest and few ancient rights or landmarks in the western part of the country. Instead, there are only different patterns of use and intensifications of occupation that mark a rhythm of open space and village, town, or city. Wherever you are, you are aware of the grid, the order, and the rhythm that made the land. Whatever sticks up in this landscape was originally made out of bricks, which is to say out of that land, and is small and expensive, as land has to be made and maintained, and so you should use as little of it as possible. Nowhere do you get any kind of broad vista without a distant church steeple or row of houses. Monuments are few and far between—they would sink back into the muck if they were too heavy.

All this made for a particular kind of architecture of grids, brick houses, and complex rhythms of open and closed that I love. But what is more important to me is that the analysis and planning of this landscape became a science. The Dutch created massive planned, private development projects centuries before anybody else did, both in cities such as Amsterdam (the "canal zone"), and in polders such as the Beemster, which was laid out as a speculative project after Amsterdam had become wealthy and is now a UNESCO World Heritage Site because it is the perfect icon of a polder. Over the centuries, a balance between private development and collective planning, later turned into government control, produced social housing of the highest quality, but it also created the notion of *ruimtelijke ordening*, or spatial arrangement.

At one point, there even was a whole ministry devoted to this notion (the Germans actually brought the term into the country when they occupied the Netherlands during World War II). Every five years or so, it did a survey of land uses and built form around the country, and then proposed how land should be reallocated between agriculture and housing, industry and culture, or just open and built. The question was not just one of what kinds of uses to build where, but also the density, height, and even character of what should be built. The same discussion happened on the local level. Thinking about the future of your society meant considering its physical form, its spaces, and its appearance.

These days spatial arrangement is out of fashion in the Netherlands, but I still hope it will come back some day. Thinking about who and where we are and where we want to be is what we should be doing in politics, planning, culture—and architecture. As Winston Churchill famously said: "We shape our buildings; thereafter they shape us." The same is true for human-made landscapes and cities.

HOW TO WEAVE THE NEW INTO THE OLD

33

It is for this reason that, when people asked me what I wanted to achieve in life, I would say: "Become Minister of Spatial Arrangement." Unfortunately, that position no longer exists, but I still love the idea. In my interpretation, the bias of which I readily admit, spatial arrangement is the continual and dynamic rearrangement of patterns of use and occupation based on an analysis of every aspect of the existing environment within the framework of different scenarios of population growth, taste culture, economic development, and a host of other variables.

In the concept of spatial arrangement, in other words, design is not something you do to a virgin territory in order to create perfection. Rather, it is a continual reinterpretation of a landscape we have made and use together so as to calibrate the best possible ways in which that landscape can develop.

My favorite radical use of this principle was a proposal an architecture student made to redo the area where the delta meets the ocean, around the city of Rotterdam. He suggested that a careful analysis of the value of the land, the rise of oceans, and the need for further development of both industrial and residential neighborhoods, as well as the preservation of natural areas, would lead to one logical scenario: remove the dikes, and let the area flood and return to being a true delta. The country could then build islands that would have the same area for houses, factories, and other uses, but would be separated from each other by abundant and beautiful water and marsh. This might be a fanciful extension of the idea, but one of the results of spatial arrangement is that it has produced some of the best experiments in building for sprawl I have seen anywhere in the world. Although the roots for these exurban communities go back to the 1920s and even before that to the new towns built in the polders, the vehicle for these experiments was the so called "Fourth Plan—Extra": the addendum to the "Fourth Plan for Spatial Arrangement" issued in 1991. Known by the Dutch acronym "Vinex," it established vehicles for building new communities in what had been agricultural or semi-industrial areas, with guidelines on how the land was to be used and what should be the mix of types of housing. There were no mandates for zoning certain areas, only a mandate that both nature and existing structures needed to be respected.

The best of these Vinex communities is Leidsche Rijn, laid out under the direction of planner Riek Bakker. The team adopted an approach that some of the same designers had developed for an expansion of Rotterdam more than a decade earlier, called Prinsenland. Rather than just paving over the rhythm of meadows, irrigation ditches, existing small villages, streams, and copses of trees, they figured out how to feather new development into the existing farms, houses, and even industrial sheds. The best moments are when you encounter a meadow now full of attached homes, then a meadow that has been left for the cows to graze, then another meadow turned into a community, then another meadow, perhaps with sheep on it. A stream cuts the rectangle of new streets, and the old village still serves as the commercial core. In the original plan, one section of meadows was to be surrounded by a wall of houses, leaving the area on the inside to revert to nature. Not all Vinex communities are so good.

BUT THIS NOTION THAT YOU BUILD WITH EXISTING PATTERNS AND ELABORATE ON THEM RATHER THAN JUST CREATING NEW COMMUNITIES IS OF CRUCIAL IMPORTANCE.

Just as interesting are some of the experiments in the actual housing itself. In one example, the firm MVRDV took the basic row house, which in the Netherlands is produced in a semi-automatic machine as tubes of concrete with shed roofs, and simply cut it apart. They left a few of the units on the front of the lot, then pushed one or two to the back, then brought the next set forward again. They did this on two sides of what had been a meadow. The result is that, instead of uniform rows of homes, you see clumps and even individual homes, with some having a front yard next to another house's rear yard. MVRDV then clad each cluster with a different material, using the same brick, tile, or metal panels for both the walls and the roof. The houses thus became abstractions of homes, each like a child's drawing, and each recognizable by its covering. "I live in that blue house," said one child when I visited, pointing to a bright blue metal object. "And I live in the tile one," said a second, pointing in the other direction; "but his is cooler."

By reducing those houses to their basic, most recognizable elements, and by breaking through the notion of the individual fitting neatly into a collective grid, MVRDV laid the groundwork for a way to rearrange the spaces of sprawl to make them more human in scale, placement, and image.

HOW TO SPIRAL OUT AND BACK AGAIN

34

What makes this spatial planning work—or what it has given birth to, depending on whether the chicken or egg came first—is the reduction of the architecture and design to a form of scenario-planning. This might seem like a contradiction. How can the reduction of the complexities of everyday life, with all the ins and outs of how people live, work with each other, and experience space, to numbers, graphics, and "what if" schemes produce something that responds to that life?

The answer is that it all starts with long and hard looking. In 1934, the City Planning Bureau of Amsterdam, led by the architect Cor van Eesteren, produced a plan for the city's expansion. They based their proposal on research into the patterns produced by people moving through the city: how they use transportation, how they work and play, and where they live. They also collected data on weather and geology, and on every other aspect of reality that could affect how

Amsterdam people might experience their environment. They translated that information into graphics that were easy to read. They then accepted the reality of existing landscapes, both urban and rural, and asked how the data could help them maximize the qualities of urban expansion. Their answer was to propose "lobes" that would extend existing neighborhoods from the city center while leaving areas of green between these new communities.

> Over the years, the Dutch continued their obsession with using data collection and analysis, and a careful look at physical reality, to design architecture that was an elaboration of the existing human-made and natural landscape in new forms rather than the plunking down of alien objects on the land. This approach helped give architecture a whole new dimension when the OMA, a Rotterdam-based firm founded by Rem Koolhaas and some of his friends, developed a conceptual approach to architecture. Rather than merely translating program and structure into an efficient building, they began fantasizing about what kinds of forms could emerge if you projected out the possibilities inherent in the conditions they found.

Thus the Kunsthal, a small exhibition building in Rotterdam, has a site next to one of the dikes that protects the city from the Rhine's floods. Its other side is a public park that is almost two full stories lower. OMA saw their brief not just as placing galleries in the shadow of this dike, but as creating a pathway between dike and park in a manner that would draw people into the galleries. The program included a certain amount of exhibition space and an auditorium, but, rather than placing these together, they treated that data as raw material that they could recombine.

Their "solution" is a box that perches on the dike and has a large opening about two-thirds down its front face. There, a path takes you down to the park. Along the way, you encounter a modest door. Enter, and you find yourself in the middle of an auditorium that runs counter to the slope. Walking down the aisle is the only way into the museum. Underground, you encounter the coat check and bathrooms, as well as the first gallery, the columns of which include fake trees so that the park, on whose level you now find yourself, continues inside. Ramps lead you back up, and pretty soon you have returned to the dike level in a skylit gallery. You continue up to the attic, where you find more galleries and a view of the city.

Koolhaas and his collaborators took the program and site, refused to accept the standard bias you might have on how to respond to its facts (front door on the park, main gallery in the middle, circulation separate, auditorium perhaps underground), and instead treated them as elements they could collage together in a way that would let you experience the existing site and the program as interlocking and revealing new possibilities. They rearranged space in a way that was logical, but unstable and open to different ways of exploring what was a flat landscape. They spiraled out of the known into the unknown and back again: the known, like the snake that bites its tail, comes back to bite itself.

HOW TO DO DEEP PLANNING

35

During the 1990s, designers who worked with and around OMA took this approach even further. MVRDV, the same firm that created the cut-apart houses, found themselves designing an apartment building for senior citizens (WoZoCo) in which some of the units had to be much larger because they were for people with reduced mobility or extra care needs. Rather than trying to hide those anomalies within the structure, they cantilevered the units out, so that they became both the logical translation of the square meters required and the building's signature. In another apartment building, the Silodam, the developer told them that the data collection indicated that there were twenty-seven different types of possible renters who might want to live there. So MVRDV surveyed Amsterdam, found twenty-seven different apartment types corresponding to the survey data on possible users, and collaged those existing dwellings together into the new structure.

Things really got crazy when the firm started to use the computing power offered by advances in technology. They turned to the Dutch government to collect all the planning data it had about how much housing, agriculture, industry, infrastructure, office space, and recreation area the country had (information collected regularly as part of the spatial arrangement process) and would need in the future. They then threw those figures into their computers and came out with KM3, a proposal for concentrating all the different functions in vertical layers that reorganized the whole country in stacks, instead of trying to cram everything into existing areas. They took the ground as data and refused to accept that it had to be on the ground. They took agriculture as square meters and thought it could be in the air. They imagined a country that was one giant structure, filled with open space and light as well as places to live and work, albeit not where you would expect them.

> While MVRDV—and especially one of its partners, Winy Maas, who now runs the appropriately named "Why Factory" at the Technical University of Delft and continues to spin out more or less fanciful data-driven scenarios—have kept their computer-driven collage going, other firms have used data in other ways. During the same period that KM3 appeared, Ben van Berkel, Caroline Bos, and their firm, UN Studio, developed what they called "deep planning." They dreamed of using the computer to take every bit of data they could find—from soil conditions to moisture readings, from traffic patterns to the strength of different materials, and from population statistics to economic predictions—analyze it, and spin out endless combinations, finally coming up with structures that were extrapolations of that data in a manner that would be both efficient and spatially rewarding.

The most successful application of their dream was the transit hub they designed for the city of Arnhem. Combining a bus terminal and a train station, it also sports a large parking garage for cars and another one for bicycles, as well as two office towers. These are not separate structures. Rather, there is a steel spiral at the middle of the station that acts as both a structural and circulation knot that ties together all of the functional elements, which take the shape of ramps, sloping walls, curving ceilings and streamlined slabs, into a single form. Landscape and parking, train tracks and bicycle shed, office floors and waiting areas flow together. The building coheres in a functional manner, but the experience you have is of the underlying relationship of all things. Landscape, planning, and architecture come together successfully in one knot.

WHY BLOBISM IS NOT THE STYLE OF THE CENTURY

36 It is this sort of solution that makes many architects believe that the computer will, and already has, fundamentally altered the way we make our world. To some, it is very simple. They think they can solve all the conundrums, all the disparities between landscape and place, between inside and out, between how we live and want to live, that have kept me wondering about architecture for most of my life on the most basic level and through the computer.

All life, they claim, is computational. That is to say, we exist as a combination of information embedded in our DNA. Our consciousness is a form of data analysis and collection. These fundamental relations that exist as spiraling binaries in the DNA helix are mirrored by the combinations of zeroes and ones that are at the basis of all computer code.

The writings of this movement's theoreticians can take on almost mystical dimensions. Kas Oosterhuis proclaims a belief in the organic nature of computer-based design, which he thinks is the only way to make form in a manner that is truly natural. Just as plants grow in complex patterns that maximize the inputs they receive from their environment and use that information to create the most efficient structure, so architecture should grow out of analysis and elaboration in manner that does away with the distinction between and the layering of program, structure, site, and form. It all flows together.

Patrik Schumacher, who has written several dense volumes on the mathematical as well as the theoretical basis of what he calls "parametricism," claims it is the "style of the century." There is no need to worry whether something is modern or classical, or whether a form is culturally correct.

ARCHITECTS SHOULD BE FREE TO LET THE COMPUTER ELABORATE THE BEST SCENARIOS FOR ANY GIVEN SITUATION.

As the director of Zaha Hadid Architects, one of the most sought-after firms in the world, Schumacher has had a chance to test his theory in many different situations, but, in the end, he still makes objects. They might be fluid in appearance and displace some of our preconceptions about how buildings fit together, but almost all of them are still functional stacks with doors and window that are not grown or elaborated, but constructed in more or less conventional ways.

To Schumacher, that is because society and its building practices lag behind his parametricism. He is deepening his approach by adopting the theory of affordances, developed by J. J. Gibson in his analysis of how animals use their environment. By feeding predicted flows and usages of spaces into an interactive computer model, Schumacher believes that he can create spaces that afford a variety of different uses instead of pinning people down in spaces.

For now, computer-based design has produced a style, although I am not sure it is the "style of the century." Usually called "blobism," after the way these buildings look, but also after the architect Greg Lynn's adaption of the scientific theory of blobs to architecture, it consists of curves, cantilevers, leaning structures, and other forms that escape from the straight and narrow. Go to Dubai, and you will see countless tilting towers rising into the sky. Go to Guangzhou, and you will see Zaha Hadid's curvaceous Opera House. Go almost anywhere in the world today, and you will see buildings testing the bounds of materials and structure in the architects' drive, depending on how skeptical you are, either to show how different they are, or to be as organic as possible. Much of this looks like science fiction, and perhaps architects are only now catching up with the realization that maybe we are already in a situation where science, rather than tradition or subjective human motives, shapes reality. Or they are creating their own vision of that future in which the computer becomes a tool to create a new look.

WHY YOU
SHOULDN'T BUILD

37 Some of the best architecture is not built. For centuries, architects have found inspiration in the work of projects that are theoretical, utopian, or unbuildable. They offer the perfection of utopia or the warning of dystopia. By the very nature of such visions, they cannot be built. And even if these visions do not go that far, but merely imagine a building that opens up a new way of being in space, they remain a proposal of what we should wish for if we only had the means.

In recent years, it seems as if computer technologies have advanced to such a point that almost anything we can imagine, we can build. That is not necessarily a good thing. Once something is constructed, it more often than not disappoints. Architects have to figure out where to put doors and windows, how to keep the rain out, how to circulate air (through unseemly grates), and how to find materials that fully and eternally represent their dreams. It is often better to see a building in the fuzzy haze of drawings that hide sins and accentuate spaces that might not be possible, no matter how much computing power is thrown at them.

One of the most evocative architects of the impossible was the late Lebbeus Woods. When I first encountered him, he was spending his days creating worlds out of combinations of colored pencil and pen, and explaining them in indecipherable texts in the margin. He had worked as an architect, and then as a renderer who drew the kind of images that sold skyscrapers to clients and the general public. In the late 1980s, he turned toward drawing things that were not there

and were not planned. He did not propose his architecture so much
as evoke its beauty and potential.

His first major body of work was *Centricity* (1986), a compound of
curving and splayed structures that looked like an experimental
outpost where mad scientists were doing something unspeak-
able. Nonetheless, you wanted to explore its intricacies through
Woods' drawings, which provided skewed perspectives that drew you
into their deepest recesses and spiraling heights.

Woods then progressed through two projects that are at the core
of his work. The first was *Underground Berlin* (1988), in which he
imagined a community of scientists and philosophers who listened
to and analyzed the very nature of the earth. They lived in and
expanded the underground train tunnels that had been abandoned by the division of Berlin into East and West. He called these
people "anarchitects": anarchists and architects who refused power
structures and came together to figure out how to make another world.

In *War and Architecture* (1993), the drawings took on a more ominous
tone. Woods spent time in the former Yugoslavia, then wracked
by civil war, and came back both thrilled by its Soviet architecture
and aghast at the destruction. His title and his drawings left it up
to us to decide whether the shapes, halfway between machines and
buildings, were implements of destruction or reconstruction.

All of Lebbeus Woods's work occupied this nebulous territory
of myth. As is the case in ancient Greek mythology, you are never
sure whether he is showing the past, the future, or a present in an
alternate reality. His work often looks like a warped version of the
world around us: one where walls and ground are bulging, fissuring,
and revealing places where that which is usually hidden behind

the walls, from electrical wires to air conditioning ducts, suddenly becomes an active part of the scene. You are seduced into something that refuses all the niceties of polite society. Architecture is an engine for reimagining our reality, not for making it work better.

Woods founded the Research Institute for Experimental Architecture, a group of architects and hangers-on (I was one of them) who made equally fantastical drawings or proposed that we think of architecture as an experiment. That meant not drawing either utopias or dystopias, but leaving open what the result of the experiment might be.

WHAT WAS IMPORTANT WAS NOT TO OFFER A SOLUTION, BUT TO ASK QUESTIONS IN AND THROUGH ARCHITECTURE.

There are still some architects today who pursue such experiments, although I would argue that one of the problems of the work, more often than not produced on computer, is that it has a do-one-thing-then-do-something-else quality. It is better to draw your myth, build it, model it, and see how one line and one form leads to another. In a world in which everything is measured and evaluated, and in which erasure is all too easy, the weirdness of experimental architecture is difficult to draw out.

WHY ARCHITECTS ARE BECOMING RHINO MONKEYS

38 What the computer is really doing to architecture is to make the work of designers more and more restricted in some ways, while liberating them in others.

A few years ago, I went to visit a student who was interning for a large architecture firm in New York. To my astonishment, he was designing a whole resort complex in China, as far as I could tell more or less by himself. He could do this because the computer automated the production of the forms. Once he knew the amount of square feet the client wanted, the site, and the optimal way to arrange these forms given predicted usage patterns, wind, sun, and soil conditions, and all the other data that go into deep planning, he could use his computer to optimize the buildings' basic placement and shape. He could then use rendering tools such as Rhino® and Grasshopper®— and others of which I had not even heard—to play with these forms to give them different appearances and render them in ways that made it appear as if they had already been built. His supervisor gave direction and edited his work, but this kid, clicking away on his mouse while computers whirred away in cyberspace, was producing a new town out of zeros and ones.

What that means for the profession is that there will be fewer jobs drafting, and more designing. It means that the gulf between those who, all by themselves or in small teams, can envision whole new buildings and cities, and those who do not have that opportunity, will become ever greater.

THE DANGER IS THAT DESIGNERS WILL BECOME UNNECESSARY.

Already, the Google X project, which finds opportunities to use search and computation technology in new ways, has produced a prototype program that will let anybody design not just a house (there are already many cheap programs and even apps for that), but large commercial structures. Use the template that Google X gives you, and you will meet all zoning and building codes, and can make the building look like something that both the neighbors and you will like (you can show it to them in those renderings that make it look built already). The process is automatic.

That might not be so good for the profession of architecture, which depends on protecting its license and the knowledge and skills that are supposedly embedded in that protected position, but will it be worse for the human-made world we inhabit? It will make the design and building process—and, if everything works as planned, the buildings themselves—more efficient and more functional. It might make everything look the same but, then again, almost everything already does. "Ninety-eight percent of everything that is designed and built today is pure shit," the architect Frank Gehry has famously said, and I don't think that the computer will do much to change that percentage.

Gehry has said something else about computer modeling, though. When I visited him a few years ago, he was finally overseeing the construction of Disney Hall, a large concert venue in Los Angeles, after many years of delays. Part of the problem in the schedule and in a vastly increased budget was due to the fact that another firm had created the construction drawings for the building, whose forms were rather complex. Using conventional means, they had not been able to analyze and represent the most efficient way to build Gehry's curves and sailing forms. He took back the drawing process and used software he developed to make the working drawings. "What the computer does is make us adults," he commented to me. "In the past, we were treated like children by both clients and construction companies. Go play in your sandbox, they would tell us, let us grown-ups tell you what you really can do and how we can do it. Now we can tell them, no, this is how you are going to do it, this is how we can work it out. It is so liberating."

That is the hope embedded in computer technology. It can let people who have a conviction about what they are doing create forms that are both efficient and exciting, rooted in data and soaring into forms we thought were impossible. It can be the large-scale equivalent of collecting items into a bricolage, which these days you might do on Amazon rather than at Home Depot. The problem is that everybody has the same technology. How will we decide what gets built, by whom, and why?

HOW TO DO TACTICAL URBANISM

39 There are, in other words, moral and ethical dimensions to the vast power the computer has unleashed. MVRDV found this out when, in 2000–01, they designed one of their what-if scenarios, which they called Pig City. At that time the Dutch kept more such animals per head of human population than any other country in Europe. Penning them into factory-like sties and slaughtering facilities, they treated the pigs horribly, and the farms produced a tremendous amount of pollution from both animal waste and the chemicals used to maximize the animals' weight and health. MVRDV proposed moving all the farms to towers in Rotterdam's harbor, where they would be far away from human habitations, the animals would have access to light and air, and the waste could be centrally treated. A populist politician, Pim Fortuyn, who was then running a contrarian campaign for parliament, mentioned on television that he thought it was a good idea. A mentally disturbed man was prompted by this (along with several other reasons) to shoot and kill Fortuyn.

Neither scenarios nor forms are neutral. They represent choices that, even when either the computer or the genius architect says they are the optimal ones, mean that other things will not happen— like the possible banning of industrial pig farming. How do we weigh the importance of things we think are good or important, even if they are not optimal? How do we understand why we are making architecture, not just how to make it more efficient?

Certainly there is one place where the traditions of architecture still have a role to play. They can guide us by showing us how architects made decisions in the past. Architecture is, after all, a way of seeing and knowing your world before it is a way of designing buildings.

In Caracas, the firm Urban-Think Tank (now based in Zurich) came to the realization that urban planning usually gets things wrong, creating neighborhoods and apartments people do not want, while not anticipating the occupation of other areas for leisure, illicit activities, or traffic, not to mention self-built neighborhoods. Planners and politicians look at things from the outside and from the top down. The model that uses the computer to reduce all reality to data and then computes the best uses of space is just another example of outside experts looking down on a territory and deciding what is best for it and its inhabitants. Instead of following this approach, Urban-Think Tank set up a card table in one of the favelas, or self-built neighborhoods, and asked people what they wanted. They let kids draw where they worked and played. They walked around and saw how people had made use of available materials and land. They saw where there were possibilities in what already existed.

Urban-Think Tank put that information into their own program and produced not abstractions, but "heat maps" that showed how areas were being used, where there was friction, and where there was space to grow. They also used social media to connect people to each other. They made movies and posted them on those same social sites. They also made proposals for buildings and pieces of infrastructure, but their main lesson was that architecture could use technology as well as traditional knowledge to activate the skills of people willing to build their own place and to open up existing space.

I THINK THEY GOT IT RIGHT. THE COMPUTER IS NOT JUST A PLACE TO STORE DATA AND MANIPULATE IT INTO FORM.

The computer is also a way to connect and activate. I think that the real electronic frontier lies in social media. As I write this, the Pokemon Go craze has just erupted on the American scene. The appearance of virtual creatures all over the city has led people to discover whole new parts of their environment. At the same time, sex sites (together with gaming, the most powerful application of new technology) are connecting people to each other without the traditional gathering points of bars and restaurants. Gaming is creating virtual worlds in which people in Australia are inhabiting the same space as users in Alaska, often for hours and even days at a time. I have no idea how these new technologies will change how we know, use, and build our spaces, but I know they will. New landscapes are appearing, and we have to figure out how to live in them, how to mark them, and how to make them our own. What is important to me is that these social media and other sites function as technologies of human connection, however virtual; as such I think they will be better building blocks for good space that connects us to each other and our world—real or projected—than slick forms spat out by computers.

HOW EVEN A STAIRCASE CAN BE SEXY

40 For all that, I will say it again: I love the look, the feel, and the smell of a good building. There is something visceral about architecture embodied in something that you can touch, and that responds to your fingers and feet in ways that surprise you. There is a curving staircase in a library designed by Louis Kahn in Exeter, New Hampshire, in which the treads, sides, and railings are made of the same stone, but each is polished to a different degree to respond to the part of your body that comes into contact with it. It is not a cheap or efficient way to make something, but it is a deeply satisfying one. There are many other examples of such sensual enjoyments, and they can feel like guilty pleasures. That is because they are usually expensive and difficult to pull off, so that you find them in buildings reserved for or built by the rich. Occasionally, an architect will figure out how to do it with humble, left-over materials, as David Ireland and Theaster Gates have done, but we do not have enough traditions or crafts to do that as well as we can in marble and hard wood. There is a task for architecture there.

WHEN ARCHITECTURE LEAVES YOU IN AWE

41

Beyond all that, there is only awe. THAT MOMENT WHEN YOUR EYES BECOME SAUCERS, YOUR MOUTH DROPS OPEN, AND YOU FEEL NOTHING BUT WONDER, IS SOMETHING THAT ARCHITECTS DREAM OF ACHIEVING, BUT SELDOM DO. It is the only thing that justifies doing more than what is necessary, right, and efficient.

Awe is deeply and profoundly personal, though there are certain things that can trigger it. Scale changes, vistas, sequences of spaces that lead you on and then open out, materials used in a way that heightens their sensuality, and sometimes the sheer complexity of a building can produce that sense in many people.

I can talk only about my own moments of awe that have led me on through architecture, and give just a few examples. I know that a year has been good when I have had at least one such experience. When I was trying to decide whether to go to architecture school, I went wandering through the Art & Architecture Building (A&A) at Yale University. It is a concrete structure that is not beloved by all. Closed in appearance and brutal in its material, it amazed me. Its architect, Paul Rudolph (for whom it is now named), designed the structure in 1961 as a new form of academic and design fortress, a condensed castle of towers around a central keep that is a stack of drafting rooms and studios. He had the workers bush-hammer the concrete to give it a rough texture that makes you sense its strength and alien quality, reminding you that it is condensed sand, brittle and hard.

He draws you into the building through a narrow slot, and then sends you wandering through no fewer than twenty-six separate levels (there is some dispute about how to count the actual number). Connected by stairs and half-stairs, opening and closing vistas, cantilevering and bridging between the cores, the A&A's spaces are a vertical maze. I went discovering, finding myself stroking the concrete in an almost masochistic manner, winding my way through studios where I knew I didn't belong, and then finally emerging on the roof, in reality only seven floors above ground. There I found the university, the city, and the landscape laid out in front of me as my head still spun from my winding path up. It was all that complexity, that pain of passage that finally released me into exhilaration.

WHERE TO FIND A MOMENT OF ZEN IN A CITY

42 The urban equivalent of that sense of compression and release was something I experienced when I stayed in a hotel room in Shibuya, a neighborhood of Tokyo where several suburban train lines enter the city at a point where a dense area of shops, nightlife, and offices has grown up. I took a room in a triangular building right at Shibuya's core. The structure was nondescript and, when I got there, I found that my room was as well. It did not matter. It was a machine for experiencing the city at its most intense.

First, I looked down. I was right above Shibuya Crossing, a square in front of the train station where several streets come together. It often shows up in photographs that illustrate Tokyo's density, and I had a near perfect version of the bird's-eye view the photographers use from my window: as the lights for the pedestrians turned green, masses surged into the streets from every angle, moving in hordes, mixing, merging, and then emerging onto opposite sidewalks in patterns you couldn't predict. It was an urban ballet carried out every ninety seconds.

My eyes moved up the sides of the buildings. It was growing dark, and the signs that are the real architecture of not only this but all great urban squares were coming alive with colors and messages I did not fully understand. Behind them were layers of restaurants, some of them stacked ten floors high. Every surface was alive, a collage of consumption so dense it seemed to shift in front of my eyes.

On top of one of the buildings, kids were playing basketball and football. Even the roofs were completely active and in motion. Then I kept looking up, past the surrounding towers that sang of the city's ambition as well as of the imprisonment of countless office workers, and there, framed between two slabs, was Mount Fuji, its perfect shape visible in the dying light. As Shibuya went on its busy way, doing all that makes cities such places of excitement, possibility, and danger, the volcano sat there, making me feel at peace through its form.

Sometimes architecture is not what you make, but what happens in the middle of our busiest cities, when functions and forms pile up, shapes and images intersect, and then, suddenly, something breaks all those boxes, opens up, and lets in air in the same way that cranking out the corner window in the Schroeder House does.

WHERE TO DISCOVER INFINITY

43 That same sense of nature making all serene is at the heart of the Salk Institute, designed by the same Louis Kahn who created that moment of sensuality in Exeter. Back when I first visited it in La Jolla, California, before they built a visitor center that now stages your visit, you approached the Institute through a grove of trees. There was no set path, just a sense that somewhere in the low wall that faced you there was an opening. You found your way, went up a few steps and through a gate and between a copse of trees. Then there was awe. You found yourself on a plaza paved in travertine and looking toward the Pacific Ocean, its blue merging with the sky above.

Everything about the plaza draws you close to the sea, even though you cannot get there from the institute. Near the beginning of the square, the travertine opens up to a square filled with water. The small basin leads to a watercourse that runs the length of the paved rectangle before disappearing, seemingly into the ocean. On either side, the studies where the researchers have their offices stand guard, facing you with weathered wood panels, but also looking toward the ocean with you through angled concrete walls that are blank at the back and turn toward their view. The study towers are porous; they are open on the ground and second floor, giving you glimpses of the shaded world of sunken courtyards and laboratories behind. Their darkness again frames the institute's sun-facing core.

Walk to the other end of the plaza, and you will find that the water tumbles down, splits, and merges again in fountains that lead you partway down the cliff. The institute is grounded, and geometry measures every step you take and every view you have. All of it, together, deepens your first sense of wonder at stone, concrete, and water, all giving way to infinity.

THIS IS ARCHITECTURE THAT DOES NOT JUST FRAME, BUT
LAYERS, DEEPENS, AND STRENGTHENS OUR EXPERIENCE
OF SOMETHING LARGER THAN WE ARE.

WHERE TO FIND
A NEW EDEN

44 Awe in architecture comes not just from realizing that nature
is bigger and more permanent, let alone more beautiful, than anything we can make. It can come from the intricacy of architecture
itself. I can get excited by the way a beam meets a column, a floor
cantilevers over the ground, a spire reaches to the sky, or even the
way a doorknob feels (the architect Alvar Aalto was particularly
good at making my mouth drop open just because I opened a door; he
would wrap his bronze handles, curved and molded with care, with
leather that is by now worn and familiar).

BUT, ULTIMATELY, ARCHITECTURE SEEKS TO MAKE A NEW
NATURE. IT REBUILDS WHAT WE REPLACE INTO A PLACE.

It makes the world something that is our own, that we own, if only
with our senses, together. The greatest architecture would be one
aiming to be a new Eden.

The closest place I know to such paradise is the Alhambra in Spain.
Like the Greek temples, it gains its power, but in this case also its
whole identity, from its site. Originally built as a fortress on a spur
of the mountains that separate the lush valleys of Andalusia from
the rest of Spain, it developed into a pleasure garden for the

Moorish dynasties that ruled the area for several centuries until they were ousted in 1492. The mountains provide more than the drama of their ridges rising above the palace and the town spread out below its turrets. They are the source of the water that the Moors channeled down through terrace after terrace of gardens before it wound up in the core of the complex, where five major courtyards use that resource to shape, enliven, and cool an outdoors but enclosed environment.

> Enter through the deep, unrelieved walls of the fortress and emerge into that sequence of enclosures, and you experience architecture dissolving into a skeleton of columns, their surfaces carved to mimic abstract natural forms, their shafts merging into layers of arches that at times turn into a texture of ever smaller versions of themselves filling shallow domes. In the center of each courtyard is water, running in shallow lines toward pools and fountains, filling the space with its sound and its smell while cooling the air that passes over it. Tiles decorated with plant motifs and intricate geometries continue the job of making a human version of nature, while orange trees and blossoming bushes make the real texture of life present in the enclosures.

Your eye dances around the geometries. You are drawn into shade, but always look into light. Architecture and nature merge, intertwine, and become something else, a textile that evokes the tents we first wove together to make our way in and through nature. Perhaps this is our way back to Eden: by taking architecture apart, dissolving it, distending it, and weaving it together with nature so that it brings us back to the moment when, naked and alone in paradise, we first clothed and separated ourselves into a world that by now covers most of creation.

HOW TO SLICE, SLASH, AND STUN

45 At the heart of architecture, there are thus beginnings that are also where architecture ends. In the last few years, many artists have realized that they can manipulate the frames and forms we use to shelter and contain ourselves to make moments of wonder without having to squeeze them into the complexity of habitable buildings. James Turrell's "Skyspaces" are one example. They actually started as double walls he cut with the same knife's edge he used in the room in Napa in which I floated. He would light the edge from behind, so that your eye would see a glowing space on the wall behind. It was a space that did not exist, a virtual apparition of infinity that floated into your consciousness.

At the opposite end of the finesse spectrum, the artist Gordon Matta-Clark in the 1970s took a power saw to buildings, cutting lozenge-shaped and spiraling holes in them to achieve that same crack and view of the sky or the street around you that awes you with the interruption and strangeness it provides. More recently, Ólafur Elíasson has done much the same with glowing lights, sheets of glass, or orbs, and you can find countless examples of other artists reaching for that moment of otherness.

> For that is what great architecture does, and why such works of art, more than buildings, might be getting at the essence of architecture. They find a strangeness in the everyday, an "other" in the recognizable. They open up what you know and confront

you with what you do not understand. They offer vistas while bringing it all back home.

IF YOU CAN CREATE ARCHITECTURE THAT MAKES YOU AWARE OF WHERE YOU ARE, AND THROUGH THAT MAKES YOU WONDER WHAT YOU ARE, YOU WILL HAVE CREATED SOMETHING GREAT.

WHAT IS TO BE DONE

46 I have experienced a great deal of architecture and tried to learn from it as I have loved it. The conclusions I draw are tentative, though I feel them passionately, and I often change my mind. So, if any of this makes sense, use it. That was the first thing I learned when I went to architecture school: if you like it, steal it. After all, the universe of possibilities is both limited and limitless. Now that I have spent almost half a century looking at architecture, almost every new building looks familiar to me. I recognize a move, a plan, a façade, a joint, or a detail.

I have also come to recognize that we build in a standardized way, using not only the same components, but also what we know is the most efficient way of putting them together. You can choose to build with steel, concrete, or wood, or whether to cover your building with glass, wood, or some new-fangled compound, but, once you do, there are only so many ways you can make it all hang together. Those choices are further limited by the building codes to which we all have to adhere.

  In the end, a building also has to make sense to those who see and use it. That means that your design has to be, at least to a certain degree, recognizable. To architects of a conventional mind, that means making a bank look like a bank and a house like a house. To those who have even less creativity, it means copying whatever shows up in the magazines or whatever is around them.

If you are smart, you will use what you find and then make it different. Stealing is easy, and it is a good start. If there is a good move out there, an efficient way to put things together and make spaces work, you should use it. Then you should figure out how to make it better. How can you do the same thing using existing materials or with an existing building? How can you get the relationship with the landscape right? How can you make what seems like a normal space seem slightly larger or more comforting? How can you open up a view through one space to another or to the outside? How can light come in and bring your textures alive? How can you, best of all, be aware that there is something other, something else, something you cannot quite name, that turns robbery into revelation?

  It would be a small step, but that would be architecture.

A NOTE ON SOURCES

This volume does not pretend to be either an academic statement or a rigorous analysis of architecture. Rather, it is a recording of how I learned to love architecture and what I learned along the way.

I have certain texts that I turn to over and over again to guide my thinking. The first group comprises what I consider to be the five key manuscripts of 20th-century architecture (I am sorry to say that we have not seen a key text emerge in this century): Le Corbusier's *Towards a New Architecture*; Robert Venturi's *Complexity and Contradiction in Architecture*; Manfredo Tafuri's *Architecture and Utopia*; Aldo Rossi's *Scientific Autobiography*; and Rem Koolhaas's *Delirious New York*. In addition, there are other key texts I keep referring to: Adolf Loos's collected writings, *Spoken into the Void*; Sigfried Giedion's *Space, Time, and Architecture*; Lewis Mumford's *Mechanization Takes Command*; Frank Lloyd Wright's essays, in particular "The Art and Craft of the Machine"; Vincent Scully's *The Earth, the Temple, and the Gods, The Shingle Style Revisited*, and *American Architecture*; John Brinckerhoff Jackson's *A Sense of Place, a Sense of Time*; John Summerson's *Heavenly Mansions*; Svetlana Alpers's *The Art of Describing*; Michael Baxandall's *Patterns Of Intention*; Colin Rowe and Fred Koetter's *Collage City*; Reyner Banham's *Los Angeles: The Architecture of Four Ecologies*; Mike Davis's *City of Quartz*; Michel Foucault's *The Order of Things*; and Henri Lefebvre's *The Production of Space*. More recently, Peter Sloterdijk's three-volume positing of *Spheres* is also of signal importance.

I think, however, that I learn just as much from literature as I do from philosophy: the Chicago and New York of Theodore Dreiser's

Sister Carrie or the interiors of Henry James's *Spoils of Poynton*; the memories of Marcel Proust in *Remembrance of Things Past* or of Karl Ove Knausgaard in *My Struggle*; the evocation of colonial Indonesia as I grew up in the Netherlands, as described by Multatuli in *Max Havelaar*, or the panoramas that unfold in Tolstoy's *War and Peace*—to name an almost random choice of examples. Then there is the science fiction of William Gibson's trilogy of *Neuromancer*, *Count Zero*, and *Mona Lisa Overdrive*, and Ursula Le Guin's stories in particular.

> There are also the movies: science fiction, of course, such as *2001: A Space Odyssey* or the earlier *The Shape of Things to Come* and *Metropolis*; *Blade Runner*, the *Star Wars* series, and the *Matrix* trilogy; but also the movies of Michelangelo Antonioni, starting with his observations of postwar Italy and continuing with *Blow Up* and *The Passenger*; and Jacques Tati's playful versions of that same reconstruction in *Mon Oncle* and *Playtime*. I also learned to love architecture as the camera swept over grand structures in movies such as *Barry Lyndon* or *The Russian Ark*; I learned about cities from *West Side Story* and the film versions of Raymond Chandler's and Dashiell Hammett's noir novels, and about domestic scenes wrought with promise and danger in the films of Francis Ford Coppola and Ingmar Bergman, to name just two visually acute filmmakers. Then there are scenes that always remain with me: classic ones like the opening and closing of *Citizen Kane*, or the less obvious images of the construction of Western towns in *McCabe and Mrs. Miller*, or the dance hall scene in *Heaven's Gate*.

More recently, I learned to look at the inner city in *The Wire* and suburbia in *The Sopranos*, and found scenes of my past in *Transparent*.

Now what I see is mainly online, in fragments and in snippets. Still I learn by surfing and by reading sites such as Archinect, Dezeen, Architectmagazine.com, Architizer, Architect's Newspaper, Suckerpunch, and many others almost daily.

Most of all, however, I learn from my students. What they come up with on a day-to-day basis continues to astonish, trouble, and delight me. If you want to learn, teach, and the other way around.

ACKNOWLEDGMENTS

Since I was a child, I have been on a path to discover why architecture matters. The people who inspired me on this path were teachers, starting with my parents, who were both professors of literature. At Yale, where I studied as both undergraduate and graduate, several individuals disciplined my thinking and opened my mind: the great architecture historian Vincent Scully, but also George Hersey, for whom I worked as a research assistant; Robert Herbert and Robert Ferris Thompson in the art history department; Stuart Wrede, who taught us architecture history in the architecture school; Cesar Pelli, that school's dean and master of ceremony; and Frederic Jameson, who taught us contemporary literary theory and philosophy. After I graduated, I continued to learn from the likes of Kurt Forster, then at the Getty Institute; Ann Bergren, who taught and brought thinkers such as Cornell West to the Southern California Institute of Architecture (SCI-Arc), and Anthony Vidler. I benefited from debates with my sister Celia McGee, Sylvia Lavin, Sanford Kwinter, Manuel DeLanda, and Mark Wigley. Jaime Rua, then a student of law, taught me philosophy. In practice, my mentors were, first and foremost, Frank Gehry, but also Craig Hodgetts, Ming Fung, and Steven Harris. Then-young practitioners who were of great influence on me include Thom Mayne, Michael Rotondi, Eric Owen Moss, Hank Koning, Julie Eizenberg, Henry Smith-Miller, Laurie Hawkinson, the late Zaha Hadid, and, perhaps just as important, fellow students and friends such as Charles Dilworth, Phil Parker, Neil Denari,

Hani Rashid, Lise Anne Couture, Tom Buresh, Edwin Chan, Christian Hubert, Mike Davis, Joe Deegan Day, and Michael Bell. There were also figures who were both theoreticians and architects, most notably Lebbeus Woods and Lars Lerup. In a category all by himself was Frank Israel, who introduced me to both the discipline and its human ecology. When I moved to San Francisco and then Europe, my horizons widened to include art historians such as Sandy Phillips and Madelene Grynsztejn; European friends, colleagues, and practitioners including Ben van Berkel and Caroline Bos, Winy Maas, Tracy Metz, Martien de Vletter, Saskia Stein, Timo de Rijk, Cor Wagenaar, Bart Lootsma, Hans Ibelings, Jacques Herzog and Pierre de Meuron, Nigel Coates, Jose Luis Mateo, Vicente Guallart, Frank Barkow, Regina Leibinger, Louisa Hutton, Mattias Sauerbruch, and Francesco Delogu. More recently, I have been stealing ideas and benefiting from discussions with Marcin Szcelina, Ladislav Zikmund-Lerner, Shumon Basar, Oliver Wainwright, Justin McGuirk, Hubert Klumpner, and Alfredo Brillembourg. And of course my husband, Peter Christian Haberkorn, remains my best critic and reality check, while my students have been the ones who keep me going, sometimes by asking the hard questions, sometimes by just doing beautiful things. To all those who might find their ideas stolen here, my apologies; for all who might not, the same. To all those who might want to find something worth stealing here, happy hunting.

INDEX

A

Aalto, Alvar 127
Alhambra, Granada 127–28
Amateur Architecture in China 54
Amsterdam 101, 105–06, 108
Anasazi 81, 90
Angell, James Rowland 16
Art & Architecture Building (A&A),
    Yale 123–24

B

Bakker, Riek 103
Berkel, Ben van 109
Bey, Jurgen 42
Biblioteca Vasconcelos, Mexico City
    30
Bos, Caroline 109
Boullée, Étienne-Louis 31–32
bricolage 46–50, 51, 52, 53–54, 55, 57, 61,
    62, 64, 118
Brillembourg, Alfredo 44
Budapest 71

C

Canyon de Chelly 81
Capp Street House, San Francisco 58–59,
    60
Chaco Canyon 81, 82
Chartres Cathedral 69
China 43, 78, 82, 86, 116
Chipperfield, David 30, 31
Cincinnati Contemporary Arts Center
    29
Corinthian (order) 36

D

De Stijl 11
Delogu, Francesco 44, 45
Delphi 37, 80
Delta Monks 61, 62
Desmarais, Charles 29
Dharavi 49–50

Diamond Ranch School, Pomona 86
Diller Scofidio + Renfro 29, 86
Disney Hall, Los Angeles 117
Dorchester Project, Chicago 60
Doric (order) 36
Droog 51, 52
Duchamp, Marcel 66

E

Ecoisland 87
École des Beaux-Arts, Paris 38
Eek, Piet Hein 52
Eesteren, Cor van 105
Elíasson, Ólafur 129

F

Fallingwater 91
Fellowship (Taliesin) 88–89
Feng Feng 44
Finucci, Maria Cristina 44, 45
Fort Ancient culture 81
Fortuyn, Pim 119

G

Gehry, Frank 18–21, 23–24, 28–29, 117–18
Gibson, J. J. 112
Goodhue, Bertram 65
Google X 117
Great Serpent Mound, Ohio 81–82
Greece 79–80
Greenaway, Peter 98

H

Hadid, Zaha 29, 111, 112
Harkness, Edward 15–16
Harvest Maps 52–53
Herzog & de Meuron 95–96
Hillside School, Taliesin 89
Home Depot modernism 55, 57
Hopi 81
Huguenot House 61

I
IKEA 55, 57
Ionic (order) 36
Ireland, David 58–59, 61, 122

J
Jackson, J. B. 83
Jeffersonian grid 67, 83
Jiménez, Carlos 44

K
Kahn, Louis 121, 125–26
Kalach, Alberto 31–32
Klumpner, Hubert 44
KM3 108, 109
Koolhaas, Rem 29–30, 33, 106, 107
Kunsthal, Rotterdam 106

L
landscrapers 84–87
Langarita-Navarro 56
Laugier, Abbé 35–36
Le Corbusier 91–92
Leidsche Rijn 103–04
Lévi-Strauss, Claude 46–47, 50
Libeskind, Daniel 29
Lincoln, Nebraska 65
Liu, Doreen 44
Loos, Adolf 37
Lynn, Greg 112

M
Maas, Winy 109
McDonald's 64, 69
Matta-Clark, Gordon 129
Mayne, Thom 86
Medvedev, Dmitry 33–34
Memorial Quadrangle, Yale 15–17
Mesa Verde 81, 82
modernism 77, 99
Mondrian, Piet 11
Moore, Charles 97

Morphosis 86
Moscow 33
Moueix, Christian 96
Mumbai 49
Museum of Contemporary Art,
        Los Angeles 19
MVRDV 104–05, 108–09, 118–19

N
Napa Valley 60, 61, 62, 95
National Parks Service 93
Native Americans 65, 67, 89
Nebraska State Capitol 64–66, 77
neo-classicism 65, 71, 78

O
Office for Metropolitan Architecture
        (OMA) 33, 106–07, 108
Oosterhuis, Kas 111
Opera House, Guangzhou 112

P
Perkins & Wills 77
Picasso, Pablo 114
Pig City 119
polders 99–101, 103
Prague 71
Prairie School homes 84
Predock, Antoine 85–86, 95
Prinsenland 103

R
Ramakers, Renny 52
Renaissance 32, 36
Research Institute for Experimental
        Architecture 115
Rietveld, Gerrit 13
Robie House 91
Rockefeller, John D. 15
Rodia, Simon 46
Rogers, James Gamble 14–18, 25
Rotterdam 102–03, 106–07, 119

Rudolph, Paul 123
Rural Studio 53

S
Salk Institute, La Jolla 125–27
Salone del Mobile, Milan 51
Schroeder House 11–13, 18, 91, 125
Schumacher, Patrik 111–12
Scully, Vincent 69, 79–80, 82
Sejima, Kazuyo 34
Semper, Gottfried 40
Shenzhen and Hong Kong Bi-City Biennale
    of Urbanism and Architecture 43
Shibuya 124–25
shingle style 84
Skolkovo 33–35
Skyspaces 62, 129
Stone, Norah and Norman 60, 61
Stonehenge 81
Superuse Studio 52–53

T
Taliesin 5, 88–90, 91
Tantimonaco, David 45
Taos Pueblo 81, 82
Theaster Gates 60–61, 122
Timberline 93–94
Tschumi, Bernard 29
Turrell, James 62, 129

U
UN Studio 109
Urban-Think Tank 119

V
Vimercati, Giovanni 45
Vinex 103–04
Viollet-le Duc, Eugène-Étienne 40

W
Wanders, Marcel 52
Watts Tower, Los Angeles 46
Why Factory 109
William I, Prince of Orange 58
Wisconsin State Capitol 77
Woods, Lebbeus 113–15
WoZoCo 108–09
Wright, Frank Lloyd 5, 84, 87–90, 91

Y
Yale, Elihu 16, 17
Yale University 14–18, 123

AARON BETSKY is an architectural curator,
critic, educator and writer. He is dean of
the Frank Lloyd Wright School of Architecture,
Taliesin West, in Scottsdale, Arizona,
and Taliesin, in Spring Green, Wisconsin.

First published in 2017 in the United States of America
by Thames & Hudson Inc., 500 Fifth Avenue, New York,
New York 10110

www.thamesandhudson.com

Library of Congress Catalog Card Number 2016952925

ISBN 978-0-500-51908-0

Printed and bound in China by Everbest Printing Co Ltd